Aussie Yarns

By R.e. Taylor

Shadowlight Publishing
Brisbane, Queensland, Australia, 4301
© 2025 All rights are reserved. Any use or reproduction is forbidden except with the written permission of the author.

ISBN: 978-1-7638437-2-1

Dedication

This book is dedicated to all of the people of the beautiful land of Australia. I found that in the history of this country, numerous stories have been passed down as oral traditions. They add to the culture Australia has created for itself and the personality of its people. Some of the stories in this book are based on First Nation legends, and they have been written with utmost respect for the Aboriginal people and their traditions.

I would also like to thank my excellent editor, Lizzie Waterhouse, and my friends Glit and Glim. I love you and appreciate everything you did to make this book possible! I could not have done it without you!

R.e.

New South Wales's Mountain Panthers

For decades, reports of the panther being spotted throughout New South Wales have primarily been confined to the Blue Mountains. Reports became so common that, in 2013, the government ordered a commission to investigate the reports. After a suitable amount of time and debate, the commission decided that the Blue Mountain Panther was merely a product of overactive imaginations and some excellent storytelling.

Sadly, a young girl named Kirra Ingram never heard of any commission and would not have cared anyway. Kirra was born in Kahtoola, about ninety minutes east of Sydney.

While Kirra was young, she learned a lot about the wildlife and flora of her homeland. After all, both of her parents were born and raised in the Blue Mountains, so her curiosity was in her blood.

Once she became a teen, she wanted to learn more, so it was not uncommon for her and her friends to take off and spend a couple of days wandering around the rainforest.

Although she knew better, Kirra was not one to listen to the stories that everything in Australia wants to kill you. So, on one of their trips, Kirra's friends woke up to find her gone. At first, they didn't think much of it but eventually became concerned.

After a couple of hours, one of the friends said, "I think we should go look for her. " The others quickly agreed, so they set off into the forest to find the missing Kirra.

They did find a set of footprints leading away from the camp but following them was useless. They disappeared suddenly about three hundred meters from where they began. Instead of searching further, they all decided that their best course of action was to return to Katoomba and seek help.

Once they made it back, they first spoke to Kirra's parents, who notified the police and filed a missing person's report. The police told her parents that most of the time, the missing person came home on their own, and that they shouldn't worry yet, as they were sure that would be the case with Kirra. She had just wandered off and would be home soon.

Of course, the friends didn't notice the giant feline footprints in the area around the campsite, nor did they hear the growls that persuaded Kirra to go walkabout in the middle of the night. If they had seen the footprints, they would have noticed that they were exactly where Kirra's footprints had stopped.

It was clear that Kirra and the large cat had met and that something had happened.

So, after a couple of days, a search party was formed and she went to the campsite with her friends as guides. Once again, they followed Kirra's footprints, and once again, they saw where they had just ended. But this time, an older man named Birrani was with them, and he immediately saw the prints the feline left.

Burrani looked carefully at them, even touching them and smelling the soil from each print. Finally, he turned to the group, lowered his head, and spoke to them. "We are not looking for a girl," he said. I know these tracks, and if she met with what I think she met with, we are looking for remains."

Then a police officer said that he was afraid to find out, but he had to know…what it was.

"I am not sure," Burrani answered, "But if I have to make a guess, I will have to say it was a huge cat."

"We do not have big cats here," the officer said.

"We do," Burrani answered. "It is well known in this area. Everyone knows about it, but no one will admit that it might exist." Just then, they heard another growl somewhere in the distance. "I hate to suggest, but everything points to a Blue Mountain panther."

Then another sound came, which no one expected. It was the sound of a human girl, and she did not sound scared or hurt. She sounded happy.

"Kirra," someone yelled, but there was no answer. "KIRRA," they yelled again, but once again, there was no answer.

Suddenly, Burrani charged into the forest. He did have a single weapon, a hunting rifle, but he also had Aboriginal knowledge to fall back on. After all, they had survived in that land a lot longer than the Europeans, and that, he felt, gave him a better chance than the others had, and maybe he could save Kirra and bring her back.

After searching for several hours, he no longer used sounds or footprints to determine where to go. Instead, he relied on his instincts, which led him to an area with large rocks, trees, and flora to match.

Stepping in quietly, he eventually found a place where animals had been resting. All through the area were feline and human footprints, so he just knew he was in the right place. Burrani took a spot a little distance away and just waited.

Just as the sun began to set, he heard some of the vegetation cracking and breaking. Then he heard a loud growl, and he saw the largest coal-black feline he had ever seen. Four cubs of the same coloring were following her.

"I got you," he said quietly as he placed his rifle against his shoulder. At that second, he was not thinking about Kirra's welfare. He was facing a mythical legend and, if he did what he was thinking. He would have the proof.

The panther looked at him with its teeth bared, and he looked straight at the panther without a blink.

As he began to pull the trigger, he saw a movement out of the corner of his eye. So, instead of firing, he lowered the rifle and released his grip.

"Mr. Burrani," a girl's voice screamed. "Please do not kill my friend. She has done nothing wrong."

"Kirra?" Burrani asked, his voice filled with confusion. "What happened to you?"

"I went out late one night," Kirra began. "I guess I must have gotten lost, and then I twisted my ankle. I was too far away to make it back, so I thought I would sit and wait. I knew someone would find me in the morning."

Burrani said he could understand that, so Kirra continued. "

"I must have fallen asleep and, when I woke up, she had her head resting on my shoulder," she said. "I felt safe, so I came back here with her, and she fed me, gave me water, and let me rest with her children."

Then Burranbi had to sit down because the panther walked over to Kirra and began rubbing her body against the child. There was no growling or sign of viciousness. Instead, she acted as if she were a perfectly behaved kitten and Kirra was her friend.

It was not until he stood up and took a step toward Kirra that any adverse reaction occurred. As soon as he moved, the panther changed her location to be directly between Burrani and Kirra. The cat's eyes were locked on the man, and she was showing significant signs of aggression.

"Okay, I understand," Burrani said as he went back to his seat. "I would never harm her." Now he knew that the panther could never understand him, but he made it better to say it anyway.

"I have to protect them," Kirra said. "As you can see, they are friendly and would never do anything to hurt me." Then she smiled at him and then at the panther. "Honestly, I don't think they would hurt anyone unless provoked.

Burani thought about everything he had seen, and he was beginning to believe the same. These 'myths' were not described in the same way by everyone. "Kirra," we must get back to the city," Burrani said. "We must let everyone know that you are safe and what has happened here." Kirra looked at him, then at the panther and its cubs. "Kirra, I promise I will not let anything happen to your friends. I swear my life on it." Finally, she agreed.

After Kirra explained what was happening to the panther and promised to return, she turned with Burrani and began the long trip home.

Once they returned, Kirra was surrounded by her family and friends. Burrani never even slowed down. He went to a building where the tribal leaders were usually found. He was right. They were gathered to find out what had happened to the little girl.

"You are truly not going to believe this," he said. "I saw it, and I cannot believe it." He began explaining about Kirra, the panther, and the cubs she was raising. The detail he brought was enough to make even the hardest disbeliever think twice about it.

Then it was Kirra's turn. She told the same story but with so many more details. Her voice never broke, even though her eyes did water when she said how that wild creature treated her. Then, she was escorted back to her parents.

The elders discussed what they were told for nearly two months. It was hard to believe that two people could have come up with such a fantastic tale. So, it was decided that, for the time being, unless proof that the stories were indeed false were provided, they would create an area measuring thirty kilometers in every direction from the city.

One man spoke to a waiting crowd. "These creatures, these Blue Mountain Panthers, are, from this day forward, to be considered equal citizens of Katoola and are protected from any harassment or harm from any human being in the area." Then he continued, "Kirra and Burrani are heroes of this community for finding out the truth and bringing it to us."

Kirra lived to a ripe old age of seventy-nine, and every year, she made a trip into the forest to spend time with her friends from her youth. The day she died, there were echoes of growls coming from every direction…a fitting tribute to a true friend to the Panthers.

The Whales Of Eden

There is one thing that Leonard and Pamela George like to do, and that is going for long rides on the weekends. When he does, both he and his wife enjoy stopping at yard sales and flea markets on the way to see what kinds of treasures they can find. Usually, it is just bric-a-brac that someone no longer wants, so they buy it, refurbish it, and sell it online. But sometimes they find something valuable or at least interesting. That was what happened when they bought a 19th-century chest from a lady in Boydtown in New South Wales.

The chest was heavy and made of oak. It was locked, and it didn't look like anyone had even tried to open it in all the time since the original owner...whoever that was. It had iron and leather strapping and a dark patina. That made Leonard happy with his discovery since it showed age.

The two of them drove back to Merimbula. It wasn't a long drive, just a few minutes. But it seemed a lot longer because George wanted to know what was in that chest. More than once, they almost stopped along the side of the road to break it open, but they decided against it. What if they did damage to the chest, or what if they lost something that may be inside? That was too great a risk to take, so they waited.

Once they got home, Leonard and Pamela opened the chest. Inside, there were vintage clothes, some household items, and even some coins featuring Queen Victoria. Counting them, they had a face value of £34.70, but they knew that coins in such good condition would be worth a lot more for Leonard than a bundle at the bottom of the chest. Carefully, he reached in, picked up the bundle, and set it on the dining room table. The gray cloth he wrapped in the bundle was tattered and rotted. It was so bad that when he tried to unwrap it, the fabric turned to dust in his hand, but the item inside remained in pristine condition.

"What is it?" Pamela asked.

"It's a book," Leonard replied. He brushed the dust off the cover and saw that it said "Journal". Nothing else, just "Journal". However, when he opened the front cover, he saw a handwritten page.

"My name is Lacy Prielipp and I was born and raised in a whaling town in Newfoundland so, of course, I worked on a Canadian ship ever since I was fifteen, but about a year ago my life here has been different to say the least so I thought I had better write it down for my children if and when I ever get married."

This sounds interesting, Leonard thought. He wanted to put the book down, the story sounded too interesting, and he was too curious, even from that first page, to want to do anything but read more.

"I made it to Australia a couple of weeks ago. It took me this long to get settled and start work," Lacy wrote. "I have been trained since they say the whales off the coast are different than the ones we hunted back home.

A week ago, I had to go out in a longboat to see if there were any whales out in the ocean. We spent the day rowing and floating, rowing and floating, but we never saw anything other than a couple of sharks that swam by us. However, once we finished our shift, we went back to shore and were told that we had the next day off.

I slept well that night, knowing that I could relax the next day. My day off wasn't going to be like everyone else's. I just wanted to see the country. After all, I was from Canada, where it was cool most of the time, so the heat of a New South Wales summer would be fun for me.

I walked a few miles into the bush. At first, I was walking on a dirt road, but I cut off and headed out into the wild to see what this country was really all about.

I walked for quite a while when I came upon a village of black people. As I walked by, they oversaw me, and I saw a few of the women run with their children. For some reason, they were scared of me, so I didn't stop. I just walked by, but then I noticed something. One of the villagers, a boy who, I guess, was fourteen or fifteen, was following me. He was standing in the grass and keeping his distance, so I didn't do anything to scare him any more than he appeared to be.

A couple of days later, I walked the same path and, once again, he was following me. This time, though, he was closer, and he wasn't worried about staying in cover, so I figured I would talk to him.

I stopped, and he stopped at the same time. "Hello, my name is Lacy," I said. "You don't have to be afraid of me."

It worked because he walked up to me, stopping about five feet away. "My name is Warrane," he said with a big smile. "I have watched you from the beach. You are a fisherman?" I told him that, yes, I was a fisherman, and that my job was to catch fish. "I saw that," he said. "You are doing it wrong. My people have been hunting whales since the beginning of time, and you are doing it wrong."

"What are we doing wrong?" I asked, but all Warrane would say was that we would learn soon what we needed to know. Then he said nothing else. He just walked away and disappeared into the bush. "What in the hell did that mean?" I asked myself, but there was no answer, so I went back to town and went to sleep.

The next morning, we went out on the boat again, and again there were no whales to be seen. We were bored to tears and just started lunch when someone, I don't remember who, saw a large fin approaching the boat. Now, I knew that

Australia was famous for one thing, and that was the man-eating sharks in its waters. A panic started on board, but for some reason, I remained calm. Maybe I had accepted the possibility of my death, or perhaps I was just being stupid...I don't know.

Whatever it was, it began circling the boat. Each time it came around, it came in closer until its fin was brushing against the wooden hull of the ship. Suddenly, it darted away and dove into the water, but it didn't stay down long. It was just a few seconds before the water exploded about twenty feet from the bow of our tiny boat.

We were in shock as a giant black and white body rose from the waves, paused for just a second, and then crashed back down, sending out a wake that shook us so severely that we nearly went over. We were lucky when our boat rode the wave with very few problems.

I happened to glance back to shore and saw Warrane and some of the elders standing on top of a nearby hill. They were pointing and talking to each other, most likely about us and what was happening, but we had more to worry about than what they were doing.

Do not be afraid, a voice said in my head. *He is a friend to my people, and he will be a friend to you.* I recognized that voice from the couple of times we had talked. It was Warrane, and he wanted me to know something. *He will help you. I promise you that.*

Once again, the creature passed by the boat. The men were terrified, so they grabbed a couple of harpoons from under the seats and raised them to kill the animal the next time it passed. "No," I yelled as the animal passed by again, and I finally got a good look at it. "It isn't a shark...I saw hundreds of them when I was in Canada. It is a killer whale. It is not here to hurt us."

It was as if the animal had heard what I said, because it stopped swimming and raised its head out of the water. It seemed to be checking us out, but it wasn't showing any aggression. It was just looking at us. Then it did something strange. It opened its mouth wide and placed its head on the side of the boat. We didn't know what it wanted. We just patted it on our heads, and it swam back into the water.

Needless to say, we didn't stay out there any longer. It took us a while to get back to shore, and the only thing we did on the way was talk about the whale and what had happened.

I didn't even have time to climb onto the dock before Warrane was standing in front of me. "Did you see him?" Warrane asked.

"Did I see who?" I asked him.

"Old Tom," he replied. "He and his family have been helping us since the Dreamtime." Well, I had no idea what Dreamtime was, but I figured it must be important to Warrane and his people. Before I could say anything, he smiled at me and asked me if I wanted him to take me out to meet Old Tom and see if he would help us find whales. I quickly agreed to meet him, and the two of us went out at dawn the next morning,

In the morning, I was at the dock about an hour before the sun was set to rise. Warrane was already there along with the elders of his village. They were holding a mangrove raft with two paddles. "You will take this," one of the elders said. "You are dealing with our traditions, and you will not do anything to upset Old Tom or his family."

"I would never harm him or your people in any way," I promised. "I have much respect for Warrane and your people. I want you to know that."

The elders must have accepted me at my word because they allowed Warrane to place the raft into the water. I was told to sit in front of him while Warrane would be in charge of the raft and getting us out to meet Old Tom.

He did the rowing while I sat in the front. We talked all the way out. He was asking me about Canada, and I was asking about his home and his people. I think we both learned a lot about each other, and I believe that on that trip, we became friends.

It was a long trip, a lot longer than we took in our boat, but suddenly Warrane stopped rowing and smiled. "We are here," he said.

I looked around and realized that we were remarkably close to the spot we had been in the day before. Warrane said that he knew that, then he picked up the oar he was using. I had heard stories, so I was nervous as I watched him. Instead of swinging at me, he took the oar and slapped it on the water three times. Yeah, I was curious, but I knew I wasn't going to get an accurate answer. "Lacy, watch the water," Warrane said.

It wasn't long before I saw the same massive black object swimming beneath the raft.

"Is that...," I started to ask.

"Yes, Lacy, which is Old Tom," Warrane said. Then he told me to take off my boots and place my feet into the water. I did as he said, and I was shocked when I did. I could feel the skin of the animal sliding across my feet as it swam below me.

Was I scared? You're damn right I was. I heard so many stories when I was in Canada about sailors falling off a ship and being eaten by large packs of killer whales. Some of the stories came from people I worked with who killer whales had attacked, while others were passed around through legends. Honestly, I didn't know if any of them could ever be believed, but who knows? I would find out.

Old Tom circled for a while before stopping and raising his head out of the water. It was amazing. Warrane spoke to the whale, and he seemed to answer him. That lasted a couple of minutes before Warrane reached into a bag, took out a big piece of meat, and placed it right into Old Tom's mouth. "We are ready," Warrane said. "Please take the rope at the front of the raft and throw it into the water."

I did as he said, and I watched as Old Tom grabbed the rope in his teeth and began towing us farther out to sea. Within seconds, we were going faster than even the Southern Cross could. "Where are we going," I asked as I hung on for dear life.

"It is a place not far from here," Warrane answered. "Your people call it Twofold Bay." I had heard of Twofold Bay. Some of the others fished and spent their time off there. Suddenly, Old Tom stopped, released the rope and swam off.

"What's going on," I asked as I looked around. I hadn't been to that area yet and I really didn't like just floating there in the middle of nowhere.

"He will be back in a minute," Warrane said.

I watched Old Tom return with a few other whales. They were grouped in a circle, and I could see there was something inside the circle...something they were herding. When it got closer I could see that it was a humpback whale. It wasn't big and it wasn't small.

"Hang on," Warrane said as he stood up and threw a spear into the whale as Old Tom moved it past us. He must have been taught well because the whale died fairly quickly. Then he did something I didn't expect. He took a knife out and carefully cut the lips off of his prize. I looked at him and he must have seen my curiosity because he explained that the lips are the most precious part of a whale and when Old Tom and his family helped them catch whale they were offered the best of the best as a tribute. "It has been that way for generations and it helps both us and them."

Warrane and I went "fishing" a few more times, and he followed the same routine, and we always came back with a whale.

After a while, I shared what I learned from Warrane with the people who ran the fishing fleet. They didn't believe me, but one thing they knew...whenever we went out, we always brought a whale back with us, even when no one else had any luck."

That was the end of the story. Leonard checked out the rest of the pages, but there were no further mentions about Warrane or Old Tom, so both he and Pam took the book to the local historical society. "We have always heard stories about Orcas helping whalers, but we always considered them legends," the director said. However, that changed when Leonard handed her the book, and she was able to sit down and read the story. "I had heard about Warrane and a man named Prielipp, but there was no proof."

Leonard and Pamela looked at each other. Their mouths moved, but there were no audible sounds. Leonard smiled and turned to the director. "You know," he started. "I got that book at a yard sale with a bunch of other stuff. I really don't need it, so if you want it, we would be glad for you to have it." The director smiled the biggest smile she had ever had and thanked Georges.

Today, the story of the whales of Eden is more than just a legend. The book that Leonard and Pamela George found has been preserved and stored in a vault under a building in Merimbula, where historians and Aboriginal leaders may research the story and maintain Australian history for time to come.

Warrigal

There are some things that humans were never meant to see or even know about, and on an isolated continent like Australia, there are many unusual things hidden away in the outback. If they are ever found, no one knows what they will do.

In some rare cases, stories from generations long past are shared and retold over and over again, until the original tale becomes so diluted that it barely retains the same meaning as when it was first told. The Lake Bundoora Sapphire was one of those stories.

The story now is that there was a magical stone that took care of the people who handled it. It would stop illnesses, end disputes, even hatreds, and make life more pleasant for everyone involved, but sadly, that story is nowhere near the truth.

Warrigal was just a young man, maybe fifteen or sixteen years old. He was the son of a hunter and a woman who told traditional stories through her paintings on bark. Warrigal wasn't able to throw a spear as well as some of the other boys in the tribe, and his hunting skills were less than impressive, so he usually stayed with the women while the men and the other boys hunted. The elders told him he was standing guard, but Warrigal knew better.

One day, he was out walking through the bush. There was a large flock of black cockatoos playing in a tree off the side of the path. They were squawking so loudly that Warrigal had to cover his ears. He had heard them before, but never as loud as they were that day, so he decided that he wouldn't stay on the path.

Warrigal took this as a sign that he was supposed to venture outside of what he considered safe. In his mind, he felt that maybe that would give him the courage to be a man and take his place within the mob.

He walked about twenty kilometers through some of the thickest bushland in the area, and that took him a long time. He passed by trees full of giant fruit bats, rivers lined with crocs, snakes, and koalas that just looked down from their perches and watched him walk beneath. He took in every sensation, as his mind soon became faster at understanding every experience he was having.

As the sun set, Warrigal settled in for the night on top of a large rock. He had a good sleep, but in the morning, he was awakened in a way he never expected. When he awoke, he saw that a large owl was sitting gently on his chest. He knew that this species of owl could only be seen at night, so he wondered why it was out in the daylight and why it was sitting there looking at him.

"What are you doing, you crazy bird?" Warrigal asked as he raised his head from the ground. The bird just looked at him, but it didn't move. Although he tried to sit up, the weight of the owl kept him pinned to the ground. He even tried shooing the bird away, but that didn't work either, so he then asked the owl what it wanted of him.

As soon as he asked, the owl spread its wings wide and flew a little over a meter from the boy, and landed on a tree root that was sticking out of the ground. The owl settled on his new perch. It never took its eyes off Warrigal; it was apparent it wanted the boy to do something, but of course, it couldn't tell him, so it just dropped to the ground and started scratching in the dirt.

Then all of a sudden, it let loose with a loud screech and flew to a branch in a nearby tree. It continued screeching until Warrigal walked over to the spot and looked down at where the owl had been scratching. He then looked at the owl and again at the scratch marks, and eventually Warrigal figured out what he was supposed to do... he had to dig, and that was precisely what he did.

Now, I must tell you that the white man was still more than a thousand years away, so Warrigal used his traditional tools, such as stones, sticks, and his hands, to dig. It took him a couple of hours, but he finally had his hole dug. It was just about sixty centimeters deep and a meter wide.

One handful at a time, he continued digging until he found something. It was something he had never seen before: a white sapphire. He had seen sapphires before, but they were always blue or black, and they were rough stones. This one was a smooth sphere... a perfect sphere that no one could have ever created, but the spirits, as it was so perfect.

Picking the sapphire up, Warrigal held up the stone to show the owl, but it was no longer sitting in the tree. He could hear the call of the bird, but he couldn't see it anywhere. Then he remembered the stories he had been told when he was no more than seven years old. The stories are about spirits who guided the lives of his people. Then he realized that maybe, just maybe, that owl was his spirit.

Picking up the sapphire, Warrigal ran back to his family. Luckily, his great-grandfather was visiting from a mob that lived across the river. "Grandfather," Warrigal started. "An ancestral being told me to retrieve this stone."

He handed it to his great-grandfather, who looked at it carefully. He showed it to the head of the tribe, who took the stone and then looked in the direction of the big red rock, quietly asking the spirits of the rock why the boy had been chosen. "This boy is not ready for such as this," he said. "He has not even been initiated into manhood. Our ancestors have not spoken his name."

Just as he finished speaking, the owl from the tree flew in and landed on Warrigal's shoulder. The two older men knew, at that moment, that the spirits had chosen Warrigal and would have to go through this alone.

"Warrigal," the elder said after he chased several youngsters away from the area. "This was foretold by the spirits when our land was young. You have been chosen, and you must follow through with whatever the ancestral spirits dictate for you to do. Take the stone you found and hold it tightly in your left hand. Then, place your hand on your heart. Warrigal did precisely as he was told.

The older men watched as Warrigal went through a violent shaking, and he watched as the boy's eyes rolled back into his skull. As badly as he wanted to help, he knew that if he touched the boy, the spirits would be displeased, so he stood back as the boy stood alone at the base of the big red rock.

The boy's mouth was twitching, and finally, it opened wide, and a strange voice came from his mouth. "The time of the First People is running short," the voice said. "People are coming who mean to destroy you. They come from the setting and the rising sun. They will claim this land and lock your people in prisons with no walls. They will abduct your women and children, and those they take will never be seen again. The people from the sun cannot be stopped. They will not allow you to have your land, and there is nothing you can do to stop this from happening."

"What does that mean?" asked Warrigal's great-grandfather, but the head of the tribe remained silent; the spirits had spoken, and their truth was law. At that moment, Warrigal's eyes closed, and he fell to the ground. "WARRIGAL," the old man yelled as he moved over to the boy. He touched the boy. His skin was warm and moist, but nothing out of the ordinary.

Some of the boys came running from the camp when they heard the older man cry out. They watched as the boy opened his eyes and smiled. "What happened?" Warrigal asked.

"Before I tell you, open your hand," the elder said. Warrigal once again did as he was told. As his fingers opened, everyone saw that the white sapphire was gone.

"Where did it go?" Warrigal asked.

"It was meant to deliver a message," the head of the tribe replied. "The message was revealed, and now the stone doesn't need to exist any longer, so it went back to the spirits."

The owl was still perched in the nearby tree. It looked down at Warrigal, and everyone there swore that it smiled before it flew away.

Warrigal lived the rest of his life never fully understanding the message the owl spirit and the sapphire had delivered. Some of the tribes may have fought each other, but on the whole, his people were blessed.

Warrigal could use his spear and was a skilled hunter for his tribe; the land was his to hunt and fish, providing for all his tribe's needs. Still, the message that he was chosen to deliver was passed by a few, from elder to elder, but eventually it was forgotten. Some did know, but those who did, never spoke of it; the spirits would protect them...

Then the day did come when the first ships were sighted off the North Coast of this land of the dreaming and ancestral spirits, and the warning from the owl and the white sapphire came true, as the oldest living population had their land and their culture fractured in what the people from the rising and setting sun called civilization.

Alpaboolal's Carnivorous Drop Bear

I love camping, I always have, and I have camped in some of the most remote spots in the US, including the floor of the Grand Canyon, the peak of Mount McKinley, the crater of Mount St. Helens, and even just inside US territorial waters on the ice pack of the Arctic Ocean.

During all those trips, I encountered some of the most dangerous animals, including polar bears, pumas, wild hogs, and many others. Still, nothing I had ever experienced prepared me for my camping holiday in Australia.

For fun, I picked a mountain that was nearly impossible to climb to the apex. It is called Alpaboolal, and the summit is composed of a sheer granite outcropping. I had heard somewhere the rest of the mountain was relatively easy to climb... but the peak itself was pretty much unbeatable.

The Aboriginals in Australia consider Alpaboolal to be the ancestral home of the spirits. So, in addition to the peak and its many challenges, I was also fairly nervous about the Aboriginals in the area getting pissed off about my presence there... Even with all of that, I still decided to camp in a forest right near the mountain.

I arrived in Cairns, where I spent a week visiting my sister who had married an Aussie. After that, I then spent a couple of days sightseeing in the beautiful rainforests of the Daintree, and then I set my GPS to get me to 16°04'S 145°24'E. Luckily, my rental car got me there in less than a day.

I first visited Cape Tribulation and then decided to camp in a forest a fair walking distance from the base of the mountain. I wanted to explore the entire terrain and possibly discover the ways of the various inhabitants, including, if possible, the secret sacred sites of the indigenous people in the area.

After several days of exploration, I got to a new campsite I had chosen for the night. It was about six o'clock in the evening. The sun was starting to go down, but I could still see everything around me. I discovered the skeletal remains of tents and campsites.

There were cans all over the area. They weren't opened in the usual way... they were ripped apart. I also saw the bones of dogs, cats, and other animals, including some giant bones. These bones were too big to be from a dog or a cat. At long last, I started thinking clearly and realized these large bones must have belonged to a group of kangaroos. "Somebody must have been really hungry," I said out loud to myself.

I spent some time actually cleaning up the mess in this once-pristine area, including burying the bones. Luckily, it was a full moon that night, and I did have a halogen light with me. They combined to provide me with enough light to set up the camp and complete all the tasks I had to do.

There was a storm during the night. Throughout the previous day, the sky had looked black and ominous, but from what I had heard from people who had come and left before me, this weather was widespread at this time of year in Eastern Australia.

It was either months and months of drought or weeks and weeks of rain. It depended on the season. I had chosen the middle of summer to come to Australia, so... this weather was something I had to put up with.

In the morning I woke up and found I had a "house guest" and it unfortunately was not the nineteen year old girl I had been dreaming about. It was a small dog. I think it may have been some kind of dingo terrier, but I wasn't sure. It seemed quite friendly, so I gave it some of my food before I later tried shooing it away. While eating, the dog kept looking up into the trees, and the strange thing was... it kept whining and then growling at something up there. I looked up and could see nothing other than a couple of kookaburras; there was nothing else in sight. The only other thing I could see through the gum trees was the remnants of the clouds from the night before, but I didn't think the dog would be acting like that about mere clouds.

Like I said, I tried to chase the dog off, but it just wouldn't go away. That dog would take off for fifteen minutes or so and then come running back, usually with a gift of some kind. It also brought back quite a few small animals, so when he was hungry, I'd cook them up and feed them to him. Yes, I found out that the dog was a male... spayed but still a male. I started calling him Boomerang because he kept coming back, and I liked that name.

I left to head back up to the mountain around ten o'clock. Of course, Boomerang followed me. He was such a good dog. He became a friend, but a friend who never got underfoot, never pissed in your shoes, or required attention 24 hours a day like so many females I have known. Who could ask for more?

We spent many days together on the mountain. I saw so much stuff I had never seen before—trees and animals that could only be seen there, and some interesting rock formations.

One day, we were also lucky to come across some Aboriginals gathered in a group, painting at the base of the mountain. They were very hospitable people and shared their tucker with me, and over a beer, started telling me tales of the Dreamtime and of their traditional ways before the white man came and invaded their land.

I left them with great sadness in my heart, knowing that progress was not their friend. They sold their paintings for small amounts of money to dealers who made a fortune selling their artwork to millionaires and Art Galleries overseas.

As I continued to climb the mountain with Boomerang as always by my side, I came across a small stream about a quarter of the way up the slope. The water was cold and crystal clear. I couldn't see any fish in it, but the plant life around that area was more than I ever expected.

I stood there for just a minute when I heard a woman's voice coming from behind a nearby bush. I hesitated as I did not want to bother her.

"Well, don't be like that… come on over," she said. Her voice was as lovely as her face. She had long blonde hair, blue eyes, and the most sensuous lips I had ever seen. "Come on and sit down. I have been here all day with nothing but the birds and plants to talk to. It would be nice to hear a human voice again," she said, as she started laughing at her own comment. I walked over. She was terrific, and I was also tired of being alone, so it worked out well.

"My name is Emily Dickinson," she said. "No relation to the poetess." She laughed again. "I always get asked that, so I just automatically say it as soon as I introduce myself. It stops a lot of questions."

"I am sure it does," I said as I laughed along with her. Then I told her my name and that I had been visiting my sister in Cairns. As I was on holiday and had another two weeks to spare, I had decided to head to Cape Tribulation and see all that the Area had to offer.

"I have been here for almost a year," she said. "I started out studying birds, and then I heard about the Phascolarctos Cinereus Edens, and it was so interesting that I switched my research, and I am concentrating on learning more about that now."

"What is the Phasco…," I asked

"Phascolarctos Cinereus Edens," she repeated.

"Okay, what is that?" I asked.

"The common name for it is a drop bear," she said with a smile. "That does sound rather cute... doesn't it?" I agreed that it did, in fact, sound cute. Then she kept going. "It is a kind of koala that lives along the east coast. They are rare. I mean, they are scarce. The thing about them is... well, there are a couple around here."

"Cool, I hope I see one," I said.

She paused a minute before she said what she had to say. "No, you don't," she said in a grave voice. 'They are known to hide up in trees, and when someone or something walks under them, they pounce down on their victim's heads and kill them and then eat them."

"That doesn't sound like anything that should have a name like that," I said.

"Well, that might be why they have another name," she said. Her face got grave. "They are called carnivorous koalas. No one knows where they first came from, but believe me, they are around here".

I must have looked at her with some disbelief, for she quickly continued, "Now, the drop bears that attack humans and kill them, they are supposed to be just a legend... a myth, but I believe that they are real, even though no one else seems to think so."

I thought about it for a few minutes. How could those cute little animals I had seen, and even cuddled, in the Cairns Tropical Zoo be the kind of animals that would attack people? Honestly, they looked so mellow and stoned as hell when I saw them. My mind was wandering around everything I ever learned about koalas. They were known all over the world as such gentle, docile creatures. "Are you sure?" I asked. She told me that yes, she was sure, and she warned me to be careful, as drop bears were very different in nature from koalas, and to keep my eyes looking up, scanning the trees.

I told her where I was camped and invited her over for a beer that evening. She happily agreed, so I went back to my campsite with Boomerang by my side to get ready for her visit. After all, who knows, if a fellow played his cards right, he might even get lucky. As an Aussie would state, "She sure was some HOT Sheila."

As soon as we returned to camp, Boomerang started acting strangely. He started running around the site barking and growling, then suddenly he just stopped in his tracks. He was looking into the bush and growling. "Boomerang, get over here," I yelled, but he just ignored me. There was something out there that he wanted, and he wanted it badly. Then, suddenly, he ran off into the dense bush.

He was barking loudly, and then all of a sudden, his barking stopped. I thought maybe he had run off too far away and I couldn't hear him, so after taking a bit of a shave, I relaxed and listened to the eerie sounds of the Australian bush as I waited for Emily's arrival and Boomerang's return.

She showed up about an hour later. I had three torches burning, so we had plenty of light to sit and talk. Yeah, she sure was a cool-looking chick, but really, I just wanted to be her friend.

Anyway, we were sitting there drinking some beers, talking, and listening to a radio station I was picking up. It played a lot of disco garbage, but unfortunately it was the only music I could find.

We were having such a good time, just talking, when we heard a weird noise in a tree above our heads. When we looked up, a brownish-grey animal was sitting on the branch above us, and I recognized it as a very large koala.

It was looking down at us. Its mouth was open, and even in the dim light, I could see a set of sharp teeth and a muzzle covered with wet, fresh blood. Emily didn't scream or anything.

She did exactly what I was doing; she just sat there looking up at this creature.

"I have to do this," she whispered excitedly to me. I just nodded. She took out a camera, aimed it, and hit the shutter.

The second the flash went off, the animal growled and moved from its perch to another branch not too far away. It had something in its claws. Neither of us could see what it was before the creature growled again and fled deeper into the bushes. As it did, it threw what it was holding at us. As Emily stood up in fright, the object it threw landed at her feet. I immediately stood up to see what it was as I shone a light down at Emily's feet. Immediately, when we recognized what it was, Emily let out a terrified scream, and I gasped in shock.

I will never erase that picture from my mind. I was looking down at the head of dear little Boomerang. My dog had been killed and decapitated, and the rest of him most likely eaten, by this monster creature that wasn't supposed even to exist.

We stood there in shock. I was utterly shaken and felt sick to my stomach. Emily was standing there like a frozen statue.

Finally, we both managed to pull ourselves together. I insisted that either she stay with me there or I go to her camp. That way, we could protect each other from the vicious creature. Emily decided that she would stay with me and that we would take turns sleeping through the night. I took the first watch. Nothing happened, luckily. I could hear that thing moving through the trees, and a couple of times I heard it growling, but neither of us saw it again that night.

We didn't get much sleep, but in the morning, we were wide awake. The first thing I did was to bury the remains of Boomerang. He had been such a great little companion; I really was going to miss him. We did not want to leave the area yet, but were still a little fearful for our own safety, so we decided to walk through the bush, looking in every tree. That creature had to be somewhere. What we were going to do... we didn't know what, but we were going to do something.

We eventually saw it about half a kilometer from my camp. It was in a tree, sleeping. I guessed it had had its fill the night before. It was too far up to climb up and kill it... and it certainly had to be killed... so now that we knew where it was, all we had to figure out was how to destroy it.

We got back to camp, had a couple of drinks, and started talking. "Koalas, I mean real koalas, don't eat meat, do they?" I asked.

"No," replied Emily. "They are such sweet, placid creatures and can only eat 58 types of eucalyptus leaves. Their bodies could never possibly digest meat or anything else, for that matter."

"I have an idea," I said. "Now, follow my logic. If a koala can't eat anything but those leaves, and this similar species can only eat meat, then what would happen..."

"If we fed that one eucalyptus," she said as if she was reading my mind. "That might work. It might just kill it, or at least slow it down enough where we can kill it ourselves." We both agreed that we would at least try it to see if it would work.

What we decided was to obtain some eucalyptus leaves, cut them into small pieces, and add them to a kilo of kangaroo meat. Then we would hang it in the tree close to where it slept, and hope and pray that it would eat that before it came after some other animal or even us.

Between the two of us, we had everything we needed, so we put it together and silently placed the meat about ten feet from the sleeping animal. Then we went back and waited.

That night, the bushland around us was quiet... maybe too calm. We sat there. We didn't dare even talk, then suddenly we heard a small branch snap. By the time we could see it, the animal was already dropping down from the tree and aiming straight at me.

I had no time to move out of the way. Its claws dug into my neck, and I felt its teeth enter the front of my head. My eyes were covered with blood, and I couldn't see what was happening, but I could hear that thing growling and howling as its claws cut deep into my flesh; they seemed to become sharper and sharper, and a whole lot deeper. I heard Emily shouting to me that she was grabbing a tent pole. I couldn't see anything, and my hearing wasn't helping me locate her, to know exactly what she was doing. The next thing I knew I felt an aluminum rod hitting my skull as she drove it through the creature's body. The pain was too much to bear, but before I passed out, I felt that creature, that monster, fall from my head and hit the ground.

When I woke up, I was in a hospital in some town quite a distance away from Alpaboolal. Emily had apparently asked for help from my Aboriginal friends, and they very kindly had carried me straight to a local white fella's house, and he had taken me in his truck to the hospital. Emily was sitting by my bedside when I returned to the land of the living, and when I was fully awake, she showed me a picture of that carnivorous bear lying on the ground. Well, she had her proof, and I had mine.

When I was fully healed, my head, neck, and face were covered with deep, wide scars. Still, I was lucky to be alive, and with Emily's photo, we had our proof that we had survived the drop bear from hell. And naturally, we also had one hell of a story to tell.

The Newspapers had a field day writing about what had happened to us. Alpaboolal soon became even more popular as a tourist attraction, with visitors coming from all over Australia looking for another "Drop Bear".

The following year, they even made a movie about our adventure. In the film, at the end, naturally, Emily and I sailed off into the sunset together. Unfortunately, that never happened. Emily was too much of a free spirit and instead headed off to explore the migrating birds in the South Pole.

We did, though, remain lifelong friends and every year or so we went camping together in the remote areas of Australia in the hopes of finding possibly "Tasmanian Tigers, Yowies and even Bunyips". We never did, of course, find any of those exciting, mystical Australian creatures, but we had great adventures trying. I will admit, though, "Drop Bears" were certainly not on our list!

The body of the creature that had scarred me for life was preserved and is locked in a museum vault. Under an agreement between Emily and me, the body is not to be placed on exhibit until we are both dead. That way, we will still have the memories and the nightmares, but we sure won't ever have to look into those fiendish eyes ever again.

A UFO at Moore River

When I was a kid, I lived in a town just north of Perth. It was a nice place to grow up, but it was a little boring, as nothing ever happened there.

Then, when I turned eighteen, some friends and I were invited out on a friend's boat to do a bit of night fishing, swimming, drinking, and spending as much time as we could, chatting up the Sheilas on board, and just generally hanging out.

It was cloudy as hell when we left, but it cleared up as night settled in. It was so clear that we watched the International Space Station pass over. It was a blast. Then, by the time we decided to head back to shore, we were more than fifty miles out to sea.

Now there were no lights to guide us by, and our host was unfortunately far too drunk even to know in what direction he was heading. So, as none of us knew how to navigate by the stars, we set a course and, hopefully, began our return. All we could figure out was that we were west of the mouth of the Moore River... a place that we all knew, from our summer holidays spent there at the beach.

We hadn't gone far before one of the girls yelled that she saw a light on the left side of the boat, so we turned and headed toward the light. It was far away —really far away —but we kept going. The further we traveled, the brighter and more distinct the light became. We thought that if it weren't the lights from the shore, it would be lights from one of the many fishing ships that worked at sea that time of night. It could have even been a planet rising in the sky... we didn't know.

There was no shape that we could see in the dim light. It was just a blob on the horizon. Even as we got closer, we still couldn't see what it was, but we knew that it was the only way we could get any help.

While we were still about five miles away, we could see the object turn toward us. We knew it turned because we watched a blue light move from the right side of the bow light to the center, facing us. It was certainly not a planet. We all agreed on that, so it had to have been a ship. We were still traveling toward the light when we noticed that it was also moving. It was moving right at us… Thank the gods. We'd now be able to find our way home.

The faster we approached, the quicker the light sped toward us, until it was less than five hundred yards away. It was then that we could see that it wasn't a ship. It was cylindrical in shape and flew no more than twenty feet above the water's surface, but it created a huge wake in front of it. The wake hit us a long time before whatever it was got to us. When it hit us, the front of the boat was lifted cleanly out of the water. We were all thrown to the deck, and a couple of us were even thrown into the air, but as quickly as the wake hit us, it was gone, and our boat was once again riding on smooth seas. The object in the air passed over us a couple of seconds later. There was no wind from its passing, and we didn't hear any engine sounds, but as it passed, our engine died, so we were floating dead in the water.

"What in the hell was that?" I asked. No one had an answer. We knew it wasn't a plane or anything like a plane, and we knew it was traveling too fast, even for a jet. Besides that, not one of us saw any wings, so what was keeping it in the air? By the time we got back on our feet, whatever it was… it was more than twenty miles away and once again just looked like a light on the horizon.

We watched as it traveled along the horizon. It was fast. When it reached the position it was in when we first saw it, it turned and, once again, flew right at us. This time, we were ready when the wake hit. We were lying on the deck, holding on to each other. The wake hit just as it did before, but this time, when the light approached, it suddenly made a ninety-degree turn without even slowing down. It buzzed us three more times before it finally stopped about a hundred and fifty yards away from us.

All of a sudden, both ends of the cylinder changed color. Instead of the white light, we could see red, blue, and green lights revolving around... one end moving clockwise and the other moving counterclockwise.

We tried again to start the engine so we could get the hell out of there, but the engine wouldn't even begin to start. The guy whose dad owned the boat had sobered up in a hurry; he took the engine hatch off and crawled down to inspect it.

When he came back up, he said that there was nothing wrong with the engine... not a single thing. It had plenty of fuel, the oil was topped off, and the battery had a full charge. For all intents and purposes, the boat should have started right up, but it wouldn't, so we were stuck.

As I said, this vast, weird flying object was totally motionless until we saw a door open on one side of it. It was just a couple of seconds later when four balls flew from the object and headed right at our boat. The girls and one of the guys jumped into the water, but for some strange reason, I couldn't move. No matter how hard I tried, I was stuck in place. The balls formed a square around me. My eyes were locked straight ahead, but I could see three of them, and I could figure out where the other one was. Unexpectedly, their light got brighter, and then there was nothing but blackness.

The next thing I knew, I was strapped down to a table, and I was struggling to get free. It was still pitch black, but I felt a mask covering my nose and mouth. There was air blowing into it, but it didn't smell right. It had a very distinct smell of sulfur. The only thing I could hear was the sound of chirping. It sounded a lot like when trees are filled with birds and they are all chirping, but not exactly, but that was what it reminded me of.

At last, the mask was removed. I was lying on a sort of table in a large room, lit by dim blue lights, except for one, which was located directly above me. It was white and it was even brighter than any of the other lights, but despite the brightness, I could still see objects in the room. It resembled some of the operating rooms I had seen on TV, but the technology was far beyond anything I had ever seen on television. I had an idea that I knew what was going to happen. I wasn't that far off.

I ended up surrounded by whatever they were. They looked remarkably human, except for one notable difference. Their skin was a grayish blue, and their eyes looked human, but they were significantly larger than our own, and they came in many different colors. I saw blue and brown just like ours, but I also saw violet and even deep red, and there was one of the creatures whose eyes were totally white. That was the one who freaked me out the most... the one with white eyes. They were shorter than most humans. They looked as if they didn't even come up to my waist, and I am well over five feet tall.

Anyway, that one was the first one to come right over to me. It was then that I noticed that they had no mouths. The "voices" I was hearing weren't coming from a mouth. This one creature looked straight at me. There was a look in its eyes of curiosity, but I did not see any anger or hatred. It reached up and turned a valve on a console next to me. Suddenly, the air I was breathing started smelling sweeter.

As it walked away from me, the others came closer. One took a blade off a small tray and placed it against my chest. I could feel the edge, but it just felt as if someone's finger was touching me. As the blade sliced into my skin, there was no pain. I just felt a little pressure. I didn't even feel any blood running from the wound. It was just as if I were lying there and nothing was happening to me.

The next thing I knew, the chirping got even louder than it had been before. It almost sounded as if they were celebrating, but now even more so. I was able to see a reflection in one of the metal objects in the room, and what I saw shocked me. That creature was reaching into my chest. I felt him moving around inside. The next thing I knew, I was watching him pull my heart out of my chest. It wasn't pulling it hard... it was very gentle with it. I watched it in its hand. My heart was still beating, and they were all touching it, looking at it, and, I assume, talking about it. Then, after an hour or so, it placed my heart back into my chest, and then it smeared some jelly on my chest. In my mind, I assumed that they were done, but I was wrong.

It wasn't long before another creature came over. Once again, the valve was turned, and the air turned sweet. It moved down between my legs and spread them wide apart. I was able to move my head just a little so I could see what it was doing. The tips of its fingers touched my genitals, pushing my penis out of the way. Then it took a large needle and drove it into my testicle. I was scared, especially when I saw the creature drawing sperm into the syringe and putting it into a small cylinder. God only knows what they wanted it for, and that was what scared me —the not knowing.

Other experiments took place for the next couple of hours. They tested every organ I had, and every time they had to cut into me, they used that jelly on the incision. Like I said, no matter what they did to me, there was never any pain. The experiment that scared me the most was when they took a long needle and extracted cells from my optic nerve. I was able to watch as the machine moved into place. I could hear the hum as it moved the needle closer to my eye, and I saw when the needle entered my eye. There was nothing I could do. To prepare me for the test, they placed clamps on my eyes to force them to remain open, and they kept a steady stream of fluid flowing across my eyes to keep them moist. The fluid was hot, and I could feel it.

After they were done, I was taken and thrown into a soft-sided cage. The bars were not exactly solid. They were made of a kind of plasma that held an electrical charge, which I discovered on more than one occasion. I could see dozens of such cells, each one having a different species. I even saw some of my human ancestors. They were thousands of years old, but they all looked alive and healthy. I started screaming. I had a reason, even though I was being held captive, but what I wanted more than anything was to be so annoying to whoever was holding me. So they would throw me back into the boat where they had taken me from, hopefully, they would not decide to kill me instead!

One of them came to my cell. It was not looking happy to say the least. I just stood there face-to-face with it. I was not going to back down, but the more I yelled, the angrier it got until finally it took a small weapon out of its holster, and it fired at me. It didn't fire bullets; it fired a smelly, sticky fluid, and when the fluid hit my chest. It was like my body was set on fire. The pain was so bad that I fell back against the wall, holding my chest and cursing out every one of those monsters.

The creature waited ten minutes as my body shook with utter pain. Then it took the weapon back out and it shot me again, but this time it was the jelly they had used on me earlier. The pain went away, and there were no marks that I had ever been burned. When it was done, it started walking down what seemed like a hall, and the minute it did, I started screaming again. It returned and shot me again, but this time the difference was... it waited twenty minutes to put the jelly on my wounds. I started screaming, even more loudly, so this time it waited thirty minutes to save me from the unbearable pain. I was weak, but I was determined, so I went to scream again, and they must have realized that their punishment wasn't going to work. So it just gave up and went away. Of course, I kept screaming, but they weren't listening.

When feeding time came around, that same creature came back. Every "human" got a big hunk of meat. There was no way to tell what the meat was from or even how old it was, but I did see one piece, which was thrown to something in the next cell. It was covered with insect larvae and mold. You see, the thing was... the meat was raw and it smelled awful, but I learned the hard way that when you're starving, you'll pretty much eat anything. The first couple of feedings, I just threw my portion back into the hallway, but when the third feeding came around, I had to eat either or die, and I was NOT going to die... not quite yet, despite those bloody aliens!

I did everything I could to annoy these alien creatures. Although the more I did, the angrier they got, I never gave up. Finally, I was taken from my cell and escorted to a large room. I could see hundreds of those creatures standing around. Maybe this was going to be it. Perhaps I had gone too far, and they were going to put a stop to everything I was doing and kill me. I was scared stiff, and I was now regretting all I had done to annoy them.

They stripped me naked and placed me in the center of the room. Then a bright light showered down from the ceiling. My head started throbbing, and my heart started racing. I closed my eyes, and the next thing I knew, I was swallowing salt water. My arms naturally clawed as hard as they could. Those bastards were not going to drown me.

I swam up about fifteen feet until I broke the surface, and found I was right next to the boat. All of my friends were there, and they were looking over the side at me. "Where have you been?" one of them asked. I didn't answer. I was so relieved to see them; I just climbed into the boat, and a round of laughter and collapse followed.

"Where are your clothes?" another friend asked as the girls teased each other, covering their eyes.

"How long have I been gone?" I asked as I came too, and one of the girls handed me a towel, which I wrapped myself in.

"About five minutes," someone answered. "You fell overboard when we hit a big wave."

I was overjoyed to be still alive; I went around embracing them all and telling them all that had happened to me. Needless to say, not one of them believed me. They didn't remember anything at all about the lights or my being taken into the alien spaceship; nothing I could say would convince them.

Still, I know the truth; after all, I lived through it. I assure you, this was not a dream. Naturally, these days I hardly ever go out in a boat, but whenever I do, I can assure you, if I see a distant light, I make sure to steer as far away from it as possible. After all, God only knows if those creatures are out there just waiting to experiment on me again, after regretting their decision to set me free? Well, let me assure you, I still feel that torturous pain, and I sure as hell never want to find out the answer.

The Curse of the Black Opal

Jailyn Jaison loved to do two things... one was travel, and the other was shopping. According to her, the two went well together, and her house was full of the treasures she had collected on her journeys. Her prized piece was an Aztec necklace that she found in Mexico City back in 1986. She had it authenticated, and it was well over nine hundred years old, worth approximately $25,000.

Actually, although Allegheny Heights was her home, she was rarely there; she was on the road every weekend with her boyfriend, Simon, or with her sister, Janice, and her niece, Violet. Then, every year for her holidays, she would always take a trip to some exotic place. This year, she had decided on Australia after hearing all about it on the Oprah Show. She had wanted so much for Simon to share this experience with her. Still, Simon managed the Art Gallery in Allegheny Heights, and the summer brought a surge of tourists and buyers for the much-in-demand, locally created art.

Simon saw her off at the Airport with promises to Skype her daily. Her trip took her first to
Melbourne for a few days, where she stayed with an old girlfriend who had married an Aussie. They were great hosts and showed her around Melbourne, even taking her on a day trip along the Great Ocean Road, which Jailyn found to be a very memorable experience. Next was Sydney, which was all she had expected and more. After that, she visited the Queensland Gold Coast, which she found to be very similar to Miami Beach in Florida, and then proceeded to Brisbane.

There, as in all the places she visited, she hired a car and headed towards the Sunshine Coast. Naturally, she took a short detour to visit Steve Irwin's Australia Zoo and found it something she would have loved to share with Simon and her niece, Violet.

From there, she drove to the small town of Montville. On arrival, she regretted her decision not to have headed straight to the fashionable Noosa. Her time was so very short, and compared to other tourist attractions she had visited in Sydney and Melbourne, it was just a little village where the stores closed far too early and there was no nightlife whatsoever. The one thing it had, though, during the early hours of the day at least, was that their shops catered to pretty much anything a tourist could want.

Jailyn was feeling hungry when she hit the little town. The first thing she saw was a candy store at a small strip mall along the side of the road. It was down a slight hill, so she almost missed it when she drove by, but she did see it, and she stopped to pick up a kilogram of fudge and some sweet-tasting candy.

A sign towards the end of the plaza pointed to a shop called The Opal Cutter. She wandered down and entered the shop. It was full of cut opals as well as raw opals, paintings made of opals, and pretty much anything you could want made from an opal.

"I am looking for something special," Jailyn said to the store's owner.

He was an extremely friendly man, and before he showed her around his store, he told her some of the legends about opals and the people who mined them. "It is believed by many that every opal has a magical power," he said. "It can be very positive or it can be negative. Some say that they are cursed, but that is just a legend. In fact, I have been in the opal business for a long time, and I never heard of anything happening because of an opal."

Jailyn was highly interested in what he was saying, but she was also eager to see more of the specialty shops before they closed. So, while the owner was talking, her eyes darted back and forth around the store, looking for that one piece, that one special stone that she could not resist. She wanted a piece that would be totally perfect. For once, price was not a worry; Simon was extremely wealthy, and he treated her like royalty, as he had told her. "Buy a special gift in Australia for yourself, honey bun, don't worry about the cost, just have fun. Here is a credit card I ordered for you. I have put $20,000 on it, darling; it is a kind of makeup gift for me not being able to come on this trip with you. Sweetheart, just charge all that your little heart desires." Jailyn knew just how lucky she was to have Simon in her life; he took care of her in every possible way, was a great lover, a good companion, and to him, Jailyn was a Goddess.

Happily, the grateful Jailyn had no hesitation in accepting the card. After all, they were already making wedding plans, everyone in her family loved him, and she also knew Simon was the best thing that had ever happened to her.

The store owner was still talking when she spied the perfect stone she wanted. She asked to see it, and the store owner took it out of the cabinet, explaining that it was a black opal from Lightning Ridge in New South Wales. He told her that Australia supplied 90% of the world's opals and that black opals, like this one with a dark red fire, were the most valuable and highly sought after, and were only found at Lightning Ridge. Jailyn looked at the beautiful stone, with its body of black with flecks of midnight blue and deep ruby red throughout the face of the stone, but the majority of it was as black as the night when there were no lights around.

Jailyn knew this was the one memento of her trip she had to have, so she paid over 5,000 Australian dollars for the stone. Just before she left the store, the shopkeeper gave her one final warning. He basically repeated what he had said earlier, that opals can be good or they can be a negative influence. Then he bagged up the stone and she left the shop. The opal shop owner was very pleased as business had been slow that week, but now, luckily, he was $5,000 richer; he was also a little worried. He had never sold a black opal before, and he didn't really know what might happen; what if the legends were really true?

After leaving the store, Jailyn stopped at a small nearby Pub for dinner, and by the time she left the pub, she decided to skip her visit to the Sunshine Coast and head back to Brisbane. It was getting dark, and she knew she had to drive down some very tricky mountain roads to get back to Brisbane. They were very narrow and dangerous, and she had been told by the barman in the pub that many had died driving them, especially when it was cloudy. The clouds often covered the mountains, and the moisture from them made the roads extremely slippery. If it was raining, the streets were even worse. Luckily, that night it wasn't raining, so though she had to be still very careful, she hoped it might not be so bad.

On the way down, she was driving about 45 kilometers per hour. Not too fast, but too fast for the road. She made one sharp turn and was face-to-face with a huge red kangaroo. She didn't have time to stop, so she swerved, and the front of her car smashed into a metal guardrail along the side of the road. She skidded nearly 50 feet down the road, showering sparks from the front of her vehicle, and rubbing against the guardrail. Once she managed to regain control of the car, she turned off the engine and took a deep breath. She was fine, other than a cut on her forehead. The vehicle was severely damaged, but the kangaroo just hopped away.

When she got out of the car, she saw how lucky she was. Beneath her front bumper was a cliff of at least 2,000 feet. She dropped to her knees and prayed, thanking God for saving her life. It took Jailyn a few hours, but a tow truck finally arrived, and she was taken to the bottom of the mountain. She spent the night in a local Motel, and in the morning, she managed to have her rental car replaced and was back on the road again.

When she returned to her hotel room in Brisbane, she fell onto the bed; she was too tired to take out her computer, so she picked up her mobile and called Simon. They talked for about half an hour... mostly about the accident and when she was coming home. She said that she had a couple more things to do, and she would be leaving in three days. Simon was happy to hear that, and she was just as excited to say it. "Honey," she said. "I bought a real treasure yesterday just before the accident!"

"What is it?" he asked, glad that she suddenly sounded so excited.

"I found this little Opal shop," she said. "It had so many pieces of art and jewelry. I just had to buy something. Oh my darling, I used the credit card you gave me, I cannot thank you enough it is totally stunning" Jailyn was actually squirming in her seat. To her, that one little rock was nearly orgasmic.

"Well, what sort of opal is it, sweetheart?" he asked lovingly, enjoying her enthusiasm.

"A black opal," she said. "Oh, Simon, it is so beautiful. I just had to have it!"

"I bet you did," he said with a laugh, then his mood changed, and he became earnest. After giving further thought to what she had just said, he became really concerned. "Jai, when is your birthday?" he asked. She teasingly reminded him that she WAS his fiancée and he SHOULD know exactly when her birthday was.

"Just tell me," he said with a voice that was more serious than he had ever used before. She reminded him that her birthday was November 22nd, and the first word out of his mouth was, "Shit". Her reaction was less than pleasant to that word.

"What do you mean, shit?" she asked. "I never said that about YOUR birthday... did I?"

"No, no, no," he said. "Are you sure that you bought a black opal?"

"Yes, I am sure," she said.

"Shit," he said again as he took a few seconds to think about what to say next. "Darling, unless you were born in October, you should never have an opal... especially a black opal."

"Why not?" she asked with a small giggle.

"Unless an opal is your birthstone, it is bad luck to own one," he said. "As a matter of fact, it carries a strong curse with it, and owning a black one is even worse. That is used by witches to cast spells and incantations to increase the power of their magic."

"Oh, Simon darling, don't be so ridiculous, that is all such a crock," she said as she laughed out loud.

"No Hon... no it's not," he replied with more urgency. "It has been well known since ancient times that black opals are nothing but trouble." He was worried, and Jailyn could sense it. "Darling, please take that stone back to where you got it and give it back to them. Don't even try to get the money back, give it to them and get the hell out of there."

Jailyn heard what he said, but, despite his concern, she knew he would not deny her the opal if she really wanted it. Besides, he was being ridiculous, listening to old wives' tales, and she did not believe in any of that stuff!

"The stone is so pretty, Simon, I really want to keep it, come on darling, please, pretty please," she said. "Jai, you are your own woman, do as you like," Simon replied, "But babe, just for me, please return it to that shop." They talked a little longer, and Jailyn promised she would think about it. Of course, she really wasn't going to take it back, but Simon sounded so concerned, she said it just to stop him worrying. After all, she was totally convinced that there was no truth to such rubbish; it was just old wives' tales and shouldn't be believed by any sensible person.

She was supposed to leave for the States three days later, but all of a sudden, she had a feeling that she couldn't explain, so she called the airline and changed her ticket to the next morning. She had no idea why, but she had this feeling she had to do it and do it right away. No doubt Simon would be thrilled, and the thought of seeing him also thrilled her; she had not realized until this trip just how much a part of her life he had become.

Jailyn was up at 7:00 AM. She immediately called Simon, telling him of the changed schedule, and he was indeed thrilled. Her flight was scheduled for noon, and she wanted to stop at a couple of places to buy gifts before arriving at the airport. She picked up a didgeridoo and an Akubra hat for Simon, some Aussie jewelry for her sister Janice, and the coolest koala tee shirt for her niece Violet... an adorable six-year-old girl who, besides Simon, was the best thing to come into Jai's life.

By nine AM, she was finished shopping, dropped off her rental car, and headed for the Airport. Her first stop on the flight home was Hong Kong. The airport was crowded and really big. "Oh shit," she said. To herself, "This is going to be the usual waiting in long lines and just making the plane in time". She made it through immigration in good time and decided to have a bite to eat, when suddenly she heard her name called over the loudspeaker.

"Jailyn Jaison..." it said. "... Pick up the white phone at the closest gate." Jailyn immediately crossed the foyer and headed for the white phone.

When she picked up the white phone, she did as instructed, waiting until the call could be connected by a voice on the line. Suddenly, Simon was talking to her from Allegheny Heights.

"Darling, I am so relieved I managed to get you. I was hesitant to call and tell you this on the phone, but I knew you were planning to spend a few days in San Francisco. Babe, we need you here as soon as possible. The family really needs you, and I promised them I would call. My Darling, steel yourself, I have some horrible news. There was a car accident."

Jailyn started to shake visibly; she didn't like at all where this was going.

As he continued, Simon had great trouble controlling his emotions. "Janice and Violet were driving home on Route 79." His voice broke as he spoke, "Darling, I am so sorry, so sorry, but Janice never made it, she died in the ambulance on the way to the hospital."

"Oh God, no," Jailyn cried out. "Oh my God!" she felt like she was going to faint as Simon continued.

"Honey, I don't know how to say this, Violet is in... "

Suddenly, the phone went dead. Hysterically, Jailyn tried calling him back on her mobile, but it was out of charge. She tried to borrow anyone's cell phone, but she was crying so hard that she couldn't make herself understood. Two seconds later, final boarding for her flight was called. She collapsed in tears. Her sister's death was beyond her comprehension; she could not take it in. It was so unbelievable. To add to it, she did not know if Violet was alive or dead. Her knees started to crumble, and she threw up! Seeing her distress, several passengers and an airline hostess came over and helped her board the plane.

It was a long flight back; the airline did their best and arranged for her to catch the first plane to Pittsburg. They even gave her a seat in first class, but she was in total shock and couldn't eat or sleep, despite all the extra comforts; all she wanted was to be home as soon as possible.

When the plane landed in San Francisco, she managed to get Simon on the phone and learned Violet was in intensive care, and it was touch and go whether she would make it. Simon said he would meet her in Pittsburgh.

Finally, after 30 hours, she eventually landed in Pittsburgh; Simon, as always, was there waiting with open loving arms. After falling into a heap into his arms and sobbing her heart out, she went utterly numb. It was a long trip home, her thoughts racing and too many bad thoughts as Simon raced down Route 79 at speeds that would have broken the law in any country.

When she made it to their front door, her mother, father, and a couple of her brothers had been waiting at the house for her. She opened the door into the hallway, and she could hear her mother crying, and her father cursing God, asking how such a thing could have happened, and why God had turned his back on such a loving daughter as Janice.

Jailyn didn't even take the time to say hello as she stepped into the house. The first thing out of her mouth was, "How's Violet?"

Immediately, her Dad came into the hallway and took her in his arms. He had to give her the answer since no one else was in the mood to hear questions, much less answer them. "Darling," he said. "Violet is going to make it. She broke her legs in two places and dislocated her shoulder, and the doctor says she'll be spending the next few weeks in the hospital, but she is going to be okay." That relaxed Jailyn a bit; at least Violet was safe. "One good thing…" her Dad reassured her, "she doesn't remember the accident and at present the Doctor thinks it best that she doesn't know that her mother is…" Her father could not get the words out; he just stood there, tears running down his face.

"That is a good thing, I guess," Jailyn said. Simon came in with all her luggage; he set it down in the hall and then took her hand. They walked into the living room and greeted the rest of the family. Simon did his best to comfort all present, but it was not easy. Two hours later, everyone left, and Jailyn fell into Simon's arms and sobbed her eyes out. In bed that night, Jai and Simon didn't talk; they didn't even make love... they just cuddled each other tightly and, after a few hours, eventually went to sleep.

The next morning, Simon had to go to work early and left before she woke up. The alarm went off at 8:00 AM, the normal time for Jailyn to go to work. She dressed and tried to eat breakfast, but just couldn't; she could think about was seeing Violet, that was all that was on her mind. She also felt it was her duty to call her boss and let him know she was back.

He was very pleased to hear from her and asked if she could stop by as something urgent had happened at work and he needed to talk to her.

Jailyn worked as an assistant store manager at a boutique out at the Alleghany Heights Mall. Her job was to sell women's clothes. Jai loved her career; she was a great saleswoman who made her customers feel special, regardless of their age, shape, or size. Oh yes, Jai loved her job, and was so good at it that she had been promised a job as store manager once she returned from Australia. No doubt that was what her boss wanted to see her about.

She visited Violet for a couple of hours. Luckily, Violet was out of intensive care. Sadly, though, Violet kept asking why Janice had not come to visit and if her mother was okay. It took all of Jailyn's strength not to burst into tears. When they took Violet away for further tests, Jailyn left to see her boss, promising to return with Simon later in the day.

She arrived at the store at 11:30 AM. As soon as she walked into the shop, she immediately sensed something was wrong. Not one person spoke to her or even looked at her, for that matter.

"Jai, can you come into my office?" the store owner said gently.

"What's wrong with everybody?" she asked as she went into the office.

"That is what I want to speak to you about," he said as he went and sat down behind his desk. She walked over and sat down before he started talking. "I do not know why, and I am very sorry about this, but I received an email from corporate. They told me that I had to dismiss you as soon as you were back. I really don't want to do it... You are a great worker, and as you know, I am promoting you to store manager, as Cherie is leaving. Jai, I have to tell you that all the customers and staff love you, and so do I, but I'm so sorry, Jai, I have no choice. I may own this business, but I borrowed heavily to start up this franchise, and corporate owns my ass! I am so very sorry."

Jailyn's heart went up into her throat. She didn't have to work. She had family money to live on, but she enjoyed working; it gave her something to do. She didn't say a word. She did not wait for a reason, as she was so deeply hurt all she could really think of at the moment was her sister Janice. To hell with work! What she had done, she did not know, but she was too upset about her sister's death and Violet's injuries to fight with anyone. She just stood up and walked through the door and out of the shop.

On the way home, she stopped off and had a couple of drinks, and went shopping for a dress for the funeral and a pair of shoes. Usually, she handled stress with a pint of Ben & Jerry's, but that wouldn't do it today. After the loss of her sister and then her job, it was just too much to bear.

She got home about four in the afternoon. She wasn't feeling too well, so she climbed into her favorite chair and turned on the TV. It was set to CNN, so she just sat back and watched it... being too tired to get up to get the remote, which was six feet away. "A plane crashed over northern Canada today," the story started. "Flight 187 from Hong Kong crashed after an engine failure. All 147 passengers on the plane were killed on impact." She just stared at the TV. Jailyn's mind started to race as she realized that was the plane she was supposed to be on. If she had not had that uneasy feeling and changed her flight to an earlier one, she would have been on that plane. Oh, those poor people, she started to sob once again. She knew she was losing control, her emotions were running higher than normal, and her stress levels were off the charts.

    She had been sitting in the same position for over an hour when Simon got home. When he did, he found her sitting in the chair, not moving. Her eyes were glassy and glazed over, and her breathing was shallow... almost too shallow to detect, but she was alive. He immediately called 911, and an ambulance showed up 15 minutes later, and Jailyn was rushed to the hospital.

    The doctor came out to see Simon shortly after Jailyn was admitted; he asked Simon a few questions regarding Jailyn's general health and then headed back to his patient. Half an hour later, Simon was informed by the same Doctor "Mr. Myers, Miss Jaison has suffered a stroke. It isn't a very serious one, but we will know for certain after further tests tomorrow, she may have to stay with us for a couple of days," the Doctor stated "But I can assure you she will be okay. We are taking her out of intensive care and into a private room, but I would appreciate it if she didn't see anyone tonight. You can visit her in the morning." Simon thanked the doctor, and as the Doctor had assured him, Jailyn was going to be okay, he called Jailyn's parents to let them know what had happened, reassuring them that Jailyn was fine and they could visit tomorrow. After that, he went across to the other wing of the hospital to visit Violet, as he knew that Jai would have wanted him to do so.

    After also reassuring Violet that her Aunt was fine. He then called Jaylin's parents once again, with the update that he had insisted on seeing Jaylin for a few seconds and that she was sleeping soundly. He then headed for home. The moment he got in his car, he had to sit there for about 20 minutes; his hands were shaking so. He loved Jailyn, and he had nearly lost her. Thank God she was going to be okay!

Shortly after midnight, Jailyn was once again moved back into intensive care. She was hooked up to various tubes and monitors, and, as she was having seizures, she was tied to the bed so that she would not fall out. A few hours later, there was a significant improvement in her condition, and the doctors and nurses assured her that she had pulled through the worst and would be fine. However, for some reason, Jailyn knew better. She would not accept any reassurances from anyone, especially the doctors telling her that everything was going to be okay. She just whispered to them as well as she could, and when she couldn't talk, as it was too much effort, she just tried to sleep, but she couldn't; all she could think about was all that had happened and Simon's warning about the Black Opal. Why had she not listened and taken it straight back to the Opal Shop?

An hour later, Jailyn regained the strength to dictate the following note to a nurse, which was to be given to Violet on her 18th birthday. "Dearest Violet, I am, rather was, your Aunt Jai. I am so sorry about your mother. I loved her very much. This is something I have to tell you. I bought a black opal in Australia. It was said to be bad luck. I laughed at Simon when he warned me of how dangerous it was. Now I am quite certain that my purchasing that Opal was what killed your mother, and so many other bad things. I am entrusting you to eliminate this blight. You will be safe from the curse since your birthday is October 4th. Please, take it back to Australia, where I bought the stone, and return it to the Opal Cutter shop in Maleny. I am so sorry for all that has happened. I know that your mother and I will watch over you and keep you safe. I love you, Aunt Jai."

As soon as the note was finished, Jailyn Jaison looked through the open window toward heaven and took her last breath.

Simon arrived 5 minutes later and never recovered from the shock of her death. He was a destroyed man, and continued to blame himself for not being by her side, listening to the doctors, and going home that night.

On her 18th birthday, Violet was given a box by Jailyn's lawyer. Inside were the black opal and the letter. Violet read the note, and two months later, accompanied by Simon as her protector, she journeyed to Australia and did exactly what her Aunt had requested.

Violet and Simon both fell in love with Australia; they returned to Maleny with the Black Opal and discovered the Opal Cutter shop, where they met Susan and Fred Meadows, a brother and sister who were the new owners of the small opal shop.

Fate can have many twists and turns. Although the Black Opal had been unlucky for Jailyn, it was a very different story for Violet. After several visits to the Opal Shop, Violet fell madly in love with Fred Meadows.

Happily, at long last, Simon picked up the pieces of his shattered life and found a new love in Fred's sister, Susan.

Violet now lives a very happy life in Australia, and thankfully, no bad luck has ever fallen her way. She now lives in Maleny with her husband, Fred Meadows, and their three kids, and sells Opals for a living.

Simon returned to America with his wife, Susan, and over time, he found true happiness once again. He never forgets his first love, and in respect for his beloved Jailyn, even though his Birthday is in October, never accepts any opals from the generous Fred and Violet, claiming Susan and his two daughters are the only radiance he ever wants in his life.

The Tale of the Tasmanian Cave

Despite being such an isolated continent, Australia has a rich history. Starting with the Chinese and the Dutch, and continuing through to the present-day British, so much has happened that the people of Australia are proud of what their country was and what it has become. However, for all the history that is known and taught in schools, there is just as much history that has yet to be discovered.

While on holiday, two men, Gerald Harris and Jackson Andrews, decided to travel from their home in Glasgow, Scotland, to Australia. They had spent their last five years of holidays visiting the main cities of Europe, and now they wanted a new experience. Jackson had an old girlfriend living in Sydney, and she had stated that there was always a spare bedroom, in case he ever wanted to visit; he was also welcome to bring a friend, male or female. It was the perfect offer: a chance to see Sydney and its world-famous Opera House, try new foods, and possibly meet some attractive Aussie girls, while also discovering some of the country's history that wasn't in the books they had read.

They spent weeks exploring Sydney and talking to any Aussie, student, or immigrant who would sit down and share their experiences in Australia. Then they moved into the outback to talk to the stereotypical Australians, as well as some Aboriginals. They did learn a lot, but they wanted something entirely different, so they booked a flight out of Darwin and flew to Hobart in the island State of Tasmania.

From Hobart, they hired a car and drove all over the island until they reached the Ben Lomond National Park, where they found a mountain called Legges Tor. At a height of over 1,500 meters, Legges Tor is the second-highest mountain on the island... second only to Mount Ossa.

Of course, the first thing they did, even before setting up a camp, was to climb the mountain. It was a long climb, but on the way up, and again on the way back down, they saw a large number of caves and crevasses. "I have an idea," Gerald said. "After we set up camp, why don't we check out some of these caves? It might be fun!"

"You know what," Jackson agreed. "I was just thinking the same thing."

They talked about it all of the way down until they found a flat area near the base of the mountain to set up their camp. The air was so crisp and clear, quite the opposite of the coal dust filled air they had to breathe at home. The birds were chirping and squawking as loud as they could. The sounds of the Australian bush were unique, just as the Aussies themselves seemed to be, and despite all the unusual noise, it was relaxing and somehow soothing. Even when some kind of small black and white animals wandered through their camp, stealing little pieces of food they just watched and laughed.

Australia was so different to Scotland, especially at night as they relaxed around the campfire. Gerald had bought in Sydney a copy of the poems of Australia's famous bush poet, Banjo Patterson, and he read it out loud to Jackson and, soothed by the fire and the poems, they managed to fall asleep at a fairly decent time, and were awake just a few minutes after the sun crested over the peak of the mountain.

That day they set off for one of the smaller caves they saw earlier. It was behind some rocks and it was hard to get into, but when they entered it was one of the most beautiful sights they had ever seen. The walls were lined with bluish white crystals. The floors were flakes of the same material and the ceiling had stalactites that looked as if they were sculpted by a master artist and then painted by God himself.

"This is fantastic," Jackson exclaimed. "I have never seen anything like it."

"Well, that is what we are here for," Gerald declared. "To see stuff we never saw before. I think this qualifies." Then they both laughed as they started taking pictures. They spent the rest of the day going deeper and deeper into the cave. Around every turn were new wonders, and they really didn't want to leave when the day started coming to an end, but it would be dark soon so they returned to their camp and crashed out for the night.

The next day brought two more caves. In one they found fossils of some of the strange animals that lived on the island when the world was young. In the other were cave paintings that had to have been more than 20,000 years old and the paintings showed a hard life where food and even water was hard to find. Somehow these ancient people had survived in a paradise that somehow thousands of years later still remained. One thing the paintings did show was that the ancient peoples ate fish and a lot of it.

"There has to be a lake around here somewhere," Harris said. "We have to find it and get us some good fish for dinner."

Andrews checked on his phone when they got back to camp, apparently there was a lake close by, but they didn't know how far or even if there were fish still there anymore. On the third day they both decided to do some fishing. It was about a five kilometer walk to the closest lake, but it was well worth it. They caught enough fish to feed a man for a month. The biggest ones they kept. The others, they just threw back.

"I can't believe this," Jackson exclaimed excitedly. "I have never had any luck like this at home!"

"I know," Gerald replied. "It is so hard to believe. I don't know what happened to those people, but I know one thing... they didn't starve." They both laughed as they prepared and cooked their meal and settled in for the night. "Tomorrow let's check out that cave just up the slope from where we were yesterday. It looked like it could be interesting." Jackson quickly agreed and they started making plans.

That cave was even harder than the others to get to. The rocks were slick and moss covered, making travel almost impossible but they struggled and after more than a few cuts and bruises, they made it to the cave opening. It was covered with ferns and flowering tropical plants and there was a small waterfall just to the right of the entrance.

They walked in. It wasn't as deep as the others, but it was still exciting. The room was filled with rocks; there was one that got their attention as soon as they walked in. It was ten meters high and only five meters wide. There was really nothing special about it, but it immediately piqued their interest. Maybe it was the fact that the ground beneath it looked like the rock had been moved, or maybe because it looked different.... They didn't know for sure, but they wanted to know more about it.

Jackson walked over and took a closer look; there was something behind the rock. Between the two of them, they managed to loosen the rock and let it fall to the ground. As soon as it hit the ground, both of them jumped back. Their eyes were wide open and their mouths were dragging on the floor. Behind the stone was a body. Mummified and still wearing its clothes, it looked like it just died recently. Now, to find a body that well preserved in the mountains of Tasmania was extremely rare, especially considering the humidity.

They looked carefully at the outfit the body was wearing. It was strange. "Doesn't that look like armor," Jackson stated more to himself than to Gerald. Under the moss that partially covered it, you could see glints of metal. It was tarnished and rusted but it was in good shape. They could see the crest of the Catholic Church emblazoned on the armor. "This is some find," Jackson stated as he tore a silver crest from the chest plate of the armor. "We have to get this checked out," he said as he stuck the crest into his pocket. The two men then replaced the rock, packed up their campsite. They made inquiries once they got back to Hobart and heard there was a professor at once of the Universities in Brisbane, who specialized in ancient church history so they caught the next plane to Brisbane.

As soon as they got to Brisbane, after making further inquiries, they rushed over to Griffith University. There was a professor there who was renowned throughout Australia, for his knowledge of ancient church history. They hurried into his office, and before the professor could say a word they placed the crest on the man's desk. Picking it up the professor examined it carefully.

"Where did you get this," the professor asked excitedly. The two of them didn't want to tell where the discovery was or that it was in Tasmania so they made up some lie and told that to the professor.

"What is it," Gerald asked.

"It is an officer's crest," the professor said. "It is really old… I mean really old."

"How old," Gerald wasn't shy about it. He really wanted to know.

The professor took a closer look. "It is nearly 850 years old," he said. Then he kept talking. "It is a crest from an officer in the battles against Asia Minor back in the 12th Century. I would put it sometime around 1150." The two of them were shocked but it wasn't over. "It is the crest of Count Raoul the First of Vermandois. All of his soldiers wore one, but it was only the officers who wore silver. The thing was the ship carrying his troops was blown off course and was never seen again. If I remember correctly… that was in 1148." Then he asked where they found it. Again, they lied and told the same story.

Now, drink can do a lot to some people. Gerald and Jackson went out drinking to celebrate their discovery that same evening at one of the local clubs. Unfortunately, it wasn't very long before Gerald had a few too many and when he tried to pick up a woman to impress her, he told her about the discovery they had made in Tasmania. Unfortunately, she wasn't drunk and she made her living as a freelance reporter for the local newspaper, so a couple of days later, the story ran on the front page.

Before the week was over both Gerald and Jackson were brought before a government inquiry. Representatives from the federal government, the governor of Tasmania, and a representative of the Knights Templar, as well as members of the Australian Historical Society, were all present to investigate the incredible find. This time Jackson and Gerald did not lie, he told about the cave, the body and the armor, as well as the exact location of the cave.

To this day in the cave is still there and has remained untouched. The cave has been declared a national treasure and grave site which puts it under the protection of the Australian government. Other than officials and archeologists, Gerald and Jackson are the only people to have seen the inside of the cave and the man who rests there. Due to the cave being an ancient aboriginal sacred site, and also due to this discovery having vast historical repercussions on the believed European discovery of Australia by the Dutch, therefore the find for over thirty five years is top secret and is at present off limits to the general public.

Still, rumors exist, and stories are sometimes told in Australian camp side yarns of the ghost of the ancient crusader, who wanders the Australian shoreline searching for his lost ship. He is unfortunately one of the least known of the many, many legends around the country. Only a few historians, and Gerald and Jackson who are now living in a retirement home in Glasgow, know that the legend is actually true. On our shores did walk an officer of the Crusades.

Call of the Yowie

If you look at a population map of Australia, you'll see that the majority of people live in the eastern half of the country, with the major east coast population centers being Sydney and Brisbane. These cities house over six million people combined, but just a few miles away you can find tree filled mountains and rainforests, swamps and plants so thick that it is impossible to see more than a few feet into the growth.

The entire continent has existed for millions of years in isolated evolution, creating such creatures as the saltwater crocodile, kangaroo, emu, and koala. Now, 60,000 years after the first humans set foot on Australian soil, new species are being discovered every year and even more species have yet to be found.

Today, just south of Brisbane, is an area called The Gold Coast. It is a widely visited area, loved by surfers and sunbathers, as well as people just looking to get away. There is one thing that lives between Brisbane and The Gold Coast that very few people know about, except through stories mothers tell, to frighten little kids, and even fewer have seen the creature, and that creature is the Yowie.

It is said that the Yowie stands between seven and nine feet tall with long arms and legs, covered with thick fur that is colored anywhere from black to red, with even a few reports of white ones found in the northern regions of New South Wales. The tales began with the Aboriginals when they told of the Yahoo (what they called the Yowie) and the tales continued with the arrival of Captain Cook. Some of his crew reported seeing a half-man, half-ape living in the rainforests.

In 1876 a man named Clarke MacDonald was originally sent to Australia as a prisoner of the British Empire, but after serving his time as a convict, he was given his certificate of freedom. He remained in the colony as he was not able to afford to return to his home in Nottingham. He took as many odd jobs as he could, and eventually was able to purchase 20 acres of land and set up a small farm near the present town of Tin Can Bay on the Southern Coast of Queensland, near Fraser Island.

Sadly, Clarke was, after his seven year sentence as a convict, a changed man and did not take much to people anymore. He never married, never had any kids, and never socialized with any of the locals. As a matter of fact, if this story was never told, no one would have ever known he existed.

After about a year of hard work he was doing fairly well. He had a small yield of vegetables that he grew and he knew how to hunt, so meat was no problem. Clarke MacDonald was able to survive on his own and was actually quite comfortable living in isolation in the bush.

One day, while he was out hunting, he heard a strange cry off in the distance. Since he was on a heavily wooded mountainside, the sound could have been anything from the wind to some hurt animal down in the valley. He knew most of the sounds in the area, but this one was different... it was more primal, more guttural, than anything he had heard before, but it was in the distance so it didn't really bother him. The animals he was planning to hunt and eat for dinner... that was a different story. He wanted to find them and he usually did.

That day it looked like a good one for hunting, as he observed a herd of kangaroos climbing up the slopes in front of him. They weren't moving the way they usually did, they were afraid of something, but he didn't know what, and to tell the truth he didn't really care. All he had to do was wait until one of these 'roos got close and then… there was dinner. He eventually bagged one and, carrying it over his shoulders, headed home.

That night the birds were extra loud, but Clarke MacDonald didn't hear a single one of them. The sound he heard that kept coming back to him was that strange sound he had heard earlier that day, and now it would not stop echoing through his brain. He knew he had never heard it before, and he had no idea what it could be. He was still thinking about it when he fell asleep and it caused him to have strong nightmares… they were so bad that he woke up with the sweats and shaking several times.

In the morning he went back to the spot where he heard the sounds. He wasn't hunting… he had only one purpose… he wanted to find the creature, or whatever it was that made that sound.

There were plenty of birds singing and the animals he could see were acting normally. He could even see a group of kangaroos in the valley eating peacefully as if nothing had happened the day before. That is so strange, Clarke thought. They shouldn't be acting like that. They should still be at least skittish. He just watched them carefully as he walked around the area. They were even relaxed when he approached them.

In the bottom of the valley he could hear someone crying. It was soft and sounded like a little girl. He walked in the direction of the sound and, in a clearing, he found a woman and child, certainly no older than five or six, they were huddled together underneath a bush and seemed to be comforting each other.

"What are you doing here?" he asked. "This is no place for a woman and a child to be."

"Oh, sir, please help us, I don't know what to do, my husband was killed last night," the young woman said with a terrified look on her face, as Clarke moved towards her, she moved deeper into the bush keeping her child behind her. She pointed to a ridge about a half mile from where he had found her. "Oh why, oh why did this have to happen, my husband just got his ticket of leave, we were so happy, it was our chance for a new start. "

She also informed Clarke, that despite the hardship, and the bloody soldiers and greedy free settlers, her husband liked it here, so they had decided to settle on that very ridge. The soil looked good for planting, there was lots of game around for food, and they had even found a spring just down the slope. She looked at Clarke her eyes filling with tears "We were so happy and thought it such a beautiful place to raise our little Elizabeth."

"So, what happened?" Clarke said with a somewhat cold and impatient tone, "I don't have all day." Actually, he felt very sorry for the woman and he just didn't know how to handle the situation.

"My husband killed a rusa deer that he saw over by the spring. He came home bragging about it and then he set about cutting it for food when I heard the strangest noise I had ever heard. I ran outside and saw my husband and something big and fur covered was attacking him... trying to steal the 'roo. My husband immediately dropped the 'roo and started to back away, but this fiend came at him, and before he could run back into the house, this creature set in for the kill and tore him to pieces. I grabbed the spare shotgun, trying to kill the creature, but it ran down the hill with the deer and disappeared... I ran to help my husband, but it was too late."

On hearing all this, Clarke immediately, asked her what the murderous creature looked like.

"I first thought it was a man, but it was so hairy it couldn't possibly have been. It was big and very, very tall... possibly nine feet at least. It was completely covered with matted dark brown hair, it had claws and a repulsive mouth and a sharp set of teeth."

Clarke stood there in shock "I am so very sorry about your husband; thank goodness that creature ran off before he harmed you, now I could be wrong but I do not think so. I always believed that it was all native superstition, but possibly what killed your husband could have been what the natives call a Yowie; I was warned about them by some aborigines that were on a walkabout and paid me a visit. They told me that their legends spoke of a giant manlike creature who roamed the woods. They warned me to avoid them at all cost. I didn't believe them, but I guess I do now." Once again the woman burst into tears. Not used to comforting anyone, let alone a woman, all Clarke could do was pat her on the shoulder, grab her belongings and start to walk with the woman and her daughter towards his cabin.

Young Elizabeth ran up and took his hand. "Thank you," she said, as she finally smiled through her tears. At that moment, Clarke MacDonald's heart melted and he felt such a deep compassion for the mother and child, which he had not felt in years.

On the way to his cabin, he found out that the woman's name was Bethany. She was twenty four years old and she had been married since she was sixteen. She and Elizabeth had lived alone for over two years in Kent, when her husband had been found guilty of stealing a loaf of bread and shipped to New Holland.

It took six months for a letter to arrive to their home in Kent. In reading the letter, Bethany learnt that, due to her husband's friendship with a high official, he had been given a ticket of leave. Immediately Bethany and Elizabeth had boarded the first ship sailing to New Holland and happily, six months later, they once again had just begun life as a family, when this devastating tragedy happened.

Clarke and the woman and child, reached the cabin at sunset, and immediately Clarke cooked them some dinner and arranged sleeping places for each of them. Bethany slept on the bed, Elizabeth had a mattress by the fireplace, and Clark MacDonald took a blanket and pillow out and slept in the shed next to his cabin.

Sometime during the night, Clarke heard that strange animal again. This time he was sure it was not the wind. The sound was a lot closer than the night before. Whatever it was, it was near the cabin, and he was sure of that when the rocks started flying from the forest. Some of them were the size of cannon balls and they were hitting the cabin and the shed with such an impact that he could hear wood being splintered as they hit.

Clarke grabbed an axe from the side of the shed and ran for the cabin. "Stay inside," he yelled to Bethany and Elizabeth. "Don't come out no matter what you hear!"

Then, as he turned around, he saw it. It was a large black creature walking between the trees no more than fifty yards from him. He could also pick up a smell. It was rancid to say the least. Kind of like a mixture of a sweating horse and the scent of a skunk when it sprays. "Come out of there," he yelled as he started towards the creature.

As he took his first step the Yahoo turned toward him. It showed no fear. As a matter of fact, it stared at him with dark black eyes and shouted a growl that was deafening. Then, suddenly it jumped on Clarke, smashing him across the face with his arm. Clarke MacDonald was thrown backward against a tree. The pain was so bad that he thought his back was broken... fortunately it wasn't, so he slowly stood up and slashed at the Yahoo with his axe. It missed by mere inches and when it passed, the Yahoo swung its arm again... hitting him square in the chest. Out of breath, Clarke collapsed onto the ground. Then, just as suddenly as the battle started, it was over.

The Yahoo just turned and ran off into the forest, leaving Clarke MacDonald lying on the ground bleeding and gasping for a single bit of air. He stayed there the rest of the night... unable to move because of the pain he was in. The woman and the child in the cabin were so terrified they did as they had been told, they did not come out for fear of their own lives.

In the morning Bethany came out and found MacDonald on the ground. He opened his eyes as soon as her hand stroked his face. "Why didn't it kill me?" he asked. "It could of and it didn't. Why am I special?"

She didn't have the answers. All she could do was to help him to his feet and into the cabin where she bandaged him up the best she could. "I have a feeling it will be back tonight," he said as she poured him some broth from the night before.

"I hope not," she said in a frightened voice. "I have just met you, but I could not survive losing anyone else. I was so terrified that we had already lost you last night. The Lord be praised, we did not!" He reassured her that was not going to happen. Then he just sat back and relaxed for a couple of hours, but both adults knew that would not be lasting very long, no doubt that Yowie would soon be back.

As Clark finished cleaning his shotgun he lay down on his bed and Bethany and Elizabeth came over and cuddled up next to him. It was for neither his pleasure nor theirs... they just wanted to hold another human being so that they could feel safe. Soon, they fell asleep, trying to catch up on the sleep they lost the night before.

After the two of them were sound asleep, Clarke got up from the bed and walked over to a small chest he kept hidden under a floorboard. He took the box, set it on the table and opened it. Inside was a silver cross on a silk rope. The cross once belonged to his mother, but he had neither seen nor needed it in more than forty years, but tonight was special... he needed someone to talk to and that someone had to be God.

"Lord God," he said. "I have never had anyone in my life that needed my protection. Please grant me the strength to keep them safe from harm and please grant little Elizabeth good dreams and do not allow her to remember all that she has seen." Of course, there was no answer but he did feel better, more like a normal man asking. He placed the cross back into the box, replaced it under the floorboard and went back to bed. The second his body hit the bed both Bethany and Elizabeth moved closer to him... so close that he could feel their heartbeats through his night clothes.

That night the sky was clear and it was full with millions and millions of stars. The birds were singing just as they should... just as if they were meant to be nature's lullaby. When the moon came up an hour later Elizabeth was found hiding in the corner of the cabin. Although nothing was happening, she was scared beyond what a child like her should ever feel. She was shaking and crying and suddenly very scared and refused all efforts to be talked to either by her mother or Clarke. So, they wrapped a blanket around her and sat down beside her and they waited until she fell back to sleep.

That night was quiet. Bethany thought she saw something looking through the windows a couple of times, but Clarke checked it out and there was nothing... not even footprints to be found anywhere. The two of them got very little sleep despite the quietness of the evening. They just spent the night talking about everything and anything they could think of. Then, just before the sun rose, a rock hit the side of the cabin. Clarke ran out of the door and was looking at the Yahoo, who was standing less than twenty feet away.

"What do you want?" Clarke asked. His legs were shaky, but he was standing his ground as he faced the monster. The Yahoo just pounded his chest, swung his arm violently and grunted something that sounded like it was trying human speech but not quite close enough to be understood. Then the creature let out an ear-shattering scream and bounded off into the trees.

That went on for about a week. There were nightly visits, rocks thrown, sticks broken across trees, and those infernal screams. One night there was a huge noise outside the cabin. Not one of them went out to see what was happening but, in the morning, Clarke found his horse torn to shreds. Its head was still hanging from the post it had been tied to but the rest of the body was nearly gone except for some pieces spread across the area. Clarke made sure neither females saw what had occurred until he had buried all the remains, as he knew they would have been utterly terrorized.

Finally, Clarke MacDonald took his old muzzle-loader out of the shed and cleaned it up, as he was low on bullets for his rifle. It was rusted badly and it took a lot of work, but he did get it ready for use, as no doubt he would soon need it. Then he sat down by the fire to figure out how he would trap and kill the creature that had been harassing him, and especially Bethany and the child, whom he had already grown very fond of.

It took quite a while, but he did come up with an idea. He would position himself on the peak of his cabin's roof. That would put him about twelve feet in the air... far enough, he thought, to keep him safe. Once the Yahoo would approach the cabin he could fire a load of glass shards and nails that should cut the creature to pieces. "That should be justice enough to make up for Elizabeth's father and my horse as well," he muttered to himself with a very determined look came across his face. He did not tell Bethany of his plan. No doubt she would have tried to stop him, as she now depended totally on Clarke.

That night he climbed up to the roof and positioned himself where he thought it would be feasible for him to have the best possible shot he could take. Then he just waited. He heard twigs break just beyond the wood line. Several rusa passed underneath him. He wanted to take the shot and kill one of them, but he just let them go. He had a bigger target he was waiting for. He was even content for a little while as he could hear Bethany telling Elizabeth some folktales to try and get her to sleep.

At last he heard branches breaking as this big, really big, creature moved toward the cabin. As it stepped from the forest it looked at him as he raised his gun and pointed it at the creature's head. Just as MacDonald pulled the trigger the Yahoo lurched forward causing the ball to land in the ground behind it. "Damn," he yelled as he struggled to reload. Before he had the ball into the barrel the creature leapt at him, swinging his arm with all of the power it had.

The Yahoo's arm hit the roof about three feet below the apex. MacDonald watched as the blackbutt logs that made the walls shattered into splinters beneath him. The shingles flew in every direction. One hit MacDonald in the front of the head, cutting the skin all of the way to the bone.

Barely conscious and nearly blind, he fumbled with his gun, still trying to get everything right so that he could get the shot. The ball fell from his hand and rolled down the roof and onto the ground. Quickly he reached in to grab another. His hands were shaking as he placed the ball on the end of his gun and drove it in with the ramrod. Although he couldn't see the Yahoo... it was close, very close. He could smell it on the breeze. So, he lowered his gun and fired. This time he hit his mark, but it was not a fatal shot. He barely scratched the creature's head.

The Yahoo let loose with a howl as it fell to the ground. However, it did not stay on the ground long. It stood up and began pounding its massive hands into the side of the house. The logs were cracking to the point where they could barely be called logs.

Clarke could hear Elizabeth crying, and Bethany screaming, as she was trying to get her little girl somewhere safe. She had seen what that thing could do and she did not want her daughter to have to live through that again, or maybe even worse.

Still on the roof, Clarke MacDonald couldn't see, and the Yahoo's pounding was soon going to break down the walls, so as a last ditch effort he dove off of the roof, grabbing the creature around the neck and throwing it to the ground. He fought as best as he could, gouging at the creature's eyes. Their blood was mixing and the mixture was creating a smell that was worse than anything ever created by man, but every move he made took strength he didn't have, so the creature easily threw him to the ground.

It stood there for a second looking down at him. Its eyes were just narrow slits and its breathing was strong as its primal rage grew. Suddenly it reached down and picked Clarke MacDonald up with one hand. It growled as they went face to face. The Yahoo knew that it had control so it took Clarke and threw him against the wall of the house. As his body hit the ground the creature, once again, swung it arm, but this time its claws entered MacDonald's chest and cut through just as if it was melted butter and then he gasped for one final breath of air and Clarke MacDonald was gone.

Bethany ran to the door. She heard the battle and she assumed that the creature had left as it did before, but it was standing outside of the door and it was "playing" with Clarke MacDonald's body as if it was a rag doll.

"No," she screamed as she watched the scene in front of her.

Out of instinct she grabbed a piece of wood from alongside the door. She opened it and ran outside. Within a few steps she was standing directly in front of the Yahoo. She swung the wood as hard as she could. It hit the creature across its shoulders. It was a blow that should have severely injured any man, but the creature stood there and shoved it off like it was a flea bite.

The creature turned around and saw Bethany standing there with the wood still in her hand. It growled out loudly and grabbed Bethany round the neck. Its hand was so big that its fingers touched beneath the back of her. Despite the fact that her breath was quickly failing, she yelled... well, she tried to yell, "Leave my daughter alone," then she passed out.

It was as if he lost interest in Bethany. He just dropped her onto the ground and went back to beating the house into splinters. That only took a few minutes before it had a hole big enough to step through... which it did.

Elizabeth was hiding in the corner. She was crying, so the Yahoo knew right where she was. It walked through the cabin like a caged animal. It was smashing the furniture, tearing at the walls and eating everything piece of food it could find. Finally, it picked up the table that was Elizabeth's hiding place. The table was thrown across the room and smashed against a distant wall. Then it growled loud... louder than it had before.

"Please," was all Elizabeth could say between her tears.

The Yahoo reached down and grabbed the little girl. It lifted her with one hand with every intent of killing her, but, once it looked into her blue eyes and saw her tears, it just tucked her under its arms and ran off into the forest. The sound of her crying and asking for her mommy echoed through the area for quite a while until it faded into nothingness.

Bethany did not make it through the night, unable to move, she passed away still lying on the ground outside the cabin before she could find help for her beloved daughter.

Thirty years later, a hunting party found a naked thirty six year old woman running naked through the forest. Her hair was long, dirty, and knotted and her skin was cut up from running through the forests. They tracked her down and finally got her pinned down. They covered her with their jackets and carried her back to their camp. She looked like a beautiful woman but she had gone feral... completely feral.

As she lay on one of their cots, the girl opened her eyes. They saw that it was hard for her, but she was trying to speak. The only sounds they heard were just two words... Elizabeth and mommy.

The woman was eventually taken to a nunnery where she lived out her life. During that time, she never regained her humanity, and other than those two words her entire vocabulary consisted of grunts, screams and howls. She died at the age of 52, still in the nunnery. No one knew he name so her tombstone just reads "Elizabeth" with the word mommy carved beneath.

More than 100 years later the Yahoo, now called the Yowie, still roams the forest of southeast Queensland, but, over the decades, as the population grew, the Yowie has also evolved and has learnt for his own survival, he must avoid man at all cost, but the sightings and stories continue and they, most likely always will.

Writer's Note:

Since 1977 on Oxley Island, and as recently as 2013 in Bexhill, New South Wales, the Yowie has been spotted throughout Queensland and New South Wales 7 times. The community of Queanbeyan has issued a $200,000 reward for anyone who can capture and present a Yowie. As of the publication of this book --- the reward has not been claimed.

Visions from the Min Min Lights

I have a story to tell. I have tried for more than 30 years to tell it. I have hired a number of people to type it up for me, but when I started telling them what happened, they would call me crazy and leave me alone. Now, my son has bought me a microphone where I can tell the story directly into a computer and it will type it for me... no judgments... it will just type what I say. All I can say is thank God for modern technology!

Before I get started, I have to tell you one thing... I am blind! I wasn't born blind. I didn't have an accident or illness that made me blind. As I tell my story you will see what happened to my sight, and if you believe it, you will believe me.

I was eighteen and had just finished school, I didn't have a job so I decided to take a couple months and go walkabout in the Outback. I was spending a couple of days hanging out on the Northern Territory side of Lake Mackay. The area was desolate, to say the least. It was dry with very, very few plants around and even fewer people. In fact, I hadn't seen another person in at least three days, which was cool with me, as I had wanted to get away from everyone, so I did!

The nice thing was at night, I didn't light a fire or anything like that, I just lay on the dry ground and looked into the sky. Even in my wildest imagination I could not visualize a universe with so many stars. It was as if the entire sky was a carpet of white with the tiniest spots of black. The best part was when a satellite or the Space Station went over, I would watch them for a couple of minutes before they fell over the horizon and were gone for another ninety minutes.

On the fourth night, I was watching the stars as usual when the ground lit up and I could see my shadow stretching out across the sand. When I turned around there was a bright light behind me. Now, I knew it couldn't be a car or a truck. The sound of the engine would have traveled for miles, and I had not heard a thing... the light was just there!

As I watched, whatever this light was hovered for a good fifteen minutes before it broke into, I would guess, a hundred different pieces. They all flew around me. Some got so close that my hair lifted from my shoulders as they flew through. Despite all these fragments being so bright, there was absolutely no heat to them. Then, just as suddenly as they appeared, they formed back into one light again and were gone.

I have to say that I was not the kind to get scared, but that light terrified me and, little did I know, that was not going to be the last time I ran into it.

The next night I had walked to the other side of the lake. It really wasn't hard since there was no water and the lake bed was as hard as concrete. I made camp under a giant lone gum. At least there I had a little shade and the leaves blowing in the breeze made a nice sound.

That night I was looking at the stars when that bloody light came again. This time it came right up to me. It was no more than a meter from my face. When I raised my arm it would back off and then fly in again. It didn't do anything else... it just hovered and that's all. "Hello," I said to no response. I tried again, but there was nothing. Then, it suddenly got a lot brighter and my head felt like it was hit full force by a ten kilo sledge hammer.

My mind swirled for a minute before it could focus. I was seeing something I could not understand. As I looked around, I was no longer in the Australian Outback. I don't know exactly where I was but what I saw was something... it was this world all right, I was in a big city, but it was completely desolate. There were some birds flying overhead and rats scampering around my feet, but nothing else... not a building, not a river, not a dog or cat... nothing!

I could see smoke billowing from piles of debris and the air was full of something that was kind of like the old iron plants I lived by as a kid. That smell got so bad that it was pretty much unbearable. Through the smoke I could see human bodies lying all over the ground. It was sickening to see what I was seeing, but that wasn't the end of it. I watched as the ground split apart and the planet exploded. I don't know why, but I was seeing the end of humanity.

Then, as quickly as it started the visions were gone and I was staring into nothingness, nothing but pitch black. I tried to focus with my eyes and then the reality soon struck me, that light had done something to me, it had literally blinded me. I was blind, I mean not with partial vision, but totally, utterly blind. To make matters worse, I was alone in the harsh Australian outback, how was I going to survive?

After a moment of sheer panic, I realized I was not in a good place. Not in a good place is probably an understatement, I couldn't see and I was in the middle of nowhere. It could have actually been the end of the Universe as far as I was concerned.

It was still night time. I could tell because of the cool breezes blowing across my face. I had a lot of thinking to do... I had to figure out what to do once morning came, unfortunately I didn't have long to wait. It felt like it was no more than about an hour before I felt the heat of the sun blazing down on me. I knew that it rose in the east, so I started out, in that direction. Luckily I still had a spare canteen full of water, so I drank very sparingly of it, just enough to keep me going.

To protect myself from any major obstacle in my path, 'till I found something better, I kept swinging my foot, and right arm, back and forth in front of me as I walked. Naturally, I tripped over a couple rocks on the way, and I also stumbled over a tree stump, so I reached down to find a fallen branch, and found one immediately, or that is what it felt like until it shivered in my hand and I realized I had grabbed hold of a snake. Luckily, I dropped it before it bit me, even so, the experience with the snake did not deter me from searching for some sort of fallen branch that I could use as a stick to guide my way.

Before I knew it, it started to get cold, and I heard dingoes howling so I knew I must have been walking all day and now it was night again. I did have some clue I was heading east, but maybe also I was just going around in circles.

Well, at least I had survived. Then I heard the sound of a some sort of vehicle approaching, I ran towards the sound, as I did I tripped on something and went crashing down, by the time I stood up the truck or whatever it was had soon faded into the distance and I was all alone once again. I cried out in despair, but the only thing to hear me were the dingoes and they were way in the distance. Then I heard a sound very near me, and the next thing I knew I was kicked very badly in the head, I soon passed out.

When I recovered about an hour later, I felt what must have been blood flowing from my head, and I had the worst headache ever, luckily I still had half a canteen left of water. I took a sip and then passed out again. I awoke to the sun beating down on me, my flesh was burning, I knew I was badly sunburnt, my head had stopped bleeding, but I still had that horrible headache and felt dizzy, and I realized my water was running out and I had to find help or it was the end for me.

I do not know 'til this day what kicked me, I can only reckon I had been socked by a kangaroo. I had, by then covered, I reckon around 20 kilometers and had a couple more hours before lack of water sent me loco, when I heard a noise in front of me. "Is there anyone there," I yelled not expecting an answer, but luckily I got one. It was a language that I recognized even though I couldn't understand it.

"I need help," I said in a voice that was cracking. I didn't have to say anything else. I felt two men grab me and put me in the back of an old truck. The ride was rough to say the least, but during the trip I was given food, water and shade.

It was a day and a half before their rattling old truck finally arrived at its destination. I knew that they had saved my life, even though I don't think I ever saw them again to thank them for saving me.

I could hear maybe a dozen people all around me and they were all talking in that language. The next thing I knew I was carried from the truck and into a humpy. Some man began chanting and placed some herbs on my eyes and sprinkled them with water. That made my eyes feel better, but I still couldn't see.

Eventually a woman who could speak English came in and sat down next to me. "What happened," she asked. I told her about the lights and my vision and she knew exactly what I was talking about.

"You see the Min Min Lights," she said. "No one knows what they are or where they come from but you first white fella see 'em so close. You big one miracle mate." Then she went on to tell me about the Aboriginal legends of the lights and a few of the European stories. The way she described the Min Min Lights, they would come in, fly around and just leave.

"Why did they do this to me," I asked.

"I ain't no idea," she replied. "Ain't never happened before." After that, she patted my hand and got up to leave, but before she did she said in a reassuring voice. "You lucky bastard, mate, Jimmy found you. So no worries mate, our Jimmy gone off to inform white fellas you need go white fella rescue, we are not able take care here." The next day I was flown out by helicopter and placed in the local hospital over 300 miles away.

Once I recovered enough, I told my story repeatedly, but no one, other than that Aboriginal woman and her tribe believed me, so eventually I just stopped telling it. But now, after all these years, I know it is time I shared my experience with as many people as possible. The Min Min Lights, and the warning that they gave me, needs to be shared with the world. I just hope, that now I have recorded it down, that someone will believe me and take heed to what those Lights showed me. I just pray that mankind can change its ways before that vision I witnessed comes true, and all humanity that we know ceases to exist... those lights have warned us... now please listen before it is too late!

The Crows

You know, everyone who doesn't live here in Australia thinks that there are acres upon acres of kangaroos leaping through the bush, and that there are koalas in every single gum tree. Well, maybe there would be if we hadn't cleared the land.

I can assure you, that kangaroos just hopping down the street is a crock. Try to order a Fosters beer at any pub, it is just not on, and believe me Kangaroos, wallabies, wombats and platypuses are hard, if not impossible, to find anywhere where there is any kind of town! Ah, but the one creature you will find by the millions are crows. There are places where their noise is so loud that you cannot think, much less watch TV or sleep.

This story I am about to relate to you is true, and I know as it happened to me when I was eight years old and living in Eneabba in Western Australia.

It was 1976, it was just the start of spring, and it was bloody hot, I mean real hot. Now, you know how that goes. On a hot day the one thing that is sure to happen is that the three big fans cooling our classroom were going to break down, and that is exactly what they did. Since it was so hot outside the school, the teacher decided to let us open the windows. Yeah, it cooled us down by a few degrees, but unfortunately in the end that ended up being a big mistake.

Now, before I go on, I am not sure you know the superstition or not, so I am going to take a moment and tell you. The story goes that if a bird flies into your house, it means that you will have greater prosperity and you will be happy. That is, any bird in the world, except for one... if a crow flies in through an open window it means that someone is going to die. Okay, now that you know that, here's what happened.

Like I was saying it was hot, so we opened the windows. It wasn't long before flies and geckos and ants started coming in... most likely to get away from the heat. It was actually pretty fun. Our teacher gave us some time to chase the geckos. None of us caught any but it was fun anyway. Then their incessant chirping started becoming a pain so we started to try to ignore them and get back to our lessons.

It wasn't too long before birds started gathering out in the playground. I could see corellas, magpies, and crows. They stayed at the far end for a long time, but eventually one crow flew from the swings and landed on the window sill.

"You kids stay away from the bird," our teacher said as she moved toward the window. She tried swinging her arms and yelling, but the bird not only didn't leave. It flew into the room and landed on her desk.

It watched her as she walked to her desk. Amazingly, it showed no fear and, when it opened its mouth, it made the most hideous sound. As it finished, more and more crows flew in through the window and landed on our desks. After our teacher, Miss Frances, finally closed the window, twenty birds had actually flown in and landed.

Now, there were twenty-five kids in the class so five of us were luckily left alone, while the rest of the kids had a crow circling and landing on their desks. Eventually, Miss Frances sent someone down to the Principal's office and, within minutes, a group of teachers and school prefects came rushing into the room. The window was opened once again and all of those people managed to chase the birds back outside. The window was closed again and we went on with our day.

The class was supposed to go on an overnight field trip to Perth the next day, but unfortunately, I had to go to my Aunt Iona's house. I guess my grandmother came into town unannounced, and Aunt Iona and my mom decided to have a get–together for her and cook her favorite food, German

Stuffed Veal Breast. I could never stand that stuff, but I ate it anyway, and I got sick as a dog that night. I spent most of the evening, and the ride home, throwing up, cramping up, and generally just being miserable.

The next morning I was still sick. I didn't want to miss that field trip, but seriously, I was in no shape to breathe, much less have fun with my friends in a faraway city. So, in 48 degree heat, my mom kept me in my room under a thick quilt. Grandma told her that would sweat all the bad stuff out of me after a couple of hours. I guess Grandma didn't know everything. I was still sick after a full day and half the night under that thing... as a matter of fact, I felt a whole lot worse!

After three days, a bottle of medicine, and more trips to the toilet than I could ever count... I got to go back to school. Most of my class was there. One notable exception was my teacher. Miss Frances was out and there was some guy heading the class.

It was strange the entire room was silent as the new teacher started giving the lesson. That wasn't right... no... not at all. It was our job as students to provide substitutes so much hell that they would want to quit teaching forever. "What's going on," I asked the boy sitting next to me. "Why is everybody so quiet?"

"Shhhhh!" he said. So I turned and asked the same of a couple other kids, but all of them ignored me and not one of them would answer me. Finally, the teacher came over and asked me what was wrong.

"That's what I'm trying to figure out," I said.

"You haven't heard," he said. When I said I had no idea what he was talking about, he handed me a note that he quickly wrote and sent me with it to the principal's office.

When I got down there I still had no idea what was going on. I hadn't done anything wrong, well not that day anyhow. I also didn't have to sit and wait like usual, once I handed over the note, I was escorted right into the Principal's office. In the room were the principal, the school nurse, a lady I had never seen before, and the school counselor. I was told to come and sit down. As I did the principal and the nurse sat on small chairs directly in front of me while the others gathered around us.

"I know you are a big boy," the principal said to me as the nurse took my hand. I told him that yes, in fact, I was a big boy. Everyone laughed at that, but for just a second before it got serious once again. "I am just going to tell you then…" he said.

"I wish you would," I replied, hoping for another laugh.

"Okay," he said as the nurse gripped my hand tighter. "You know your class had a field trip to Perth the other day?" I did remember that even though I didn't go. "Well, after your class got back into town and the bus driver delivered everyone safely to their homes, Miss Frances was driving out on the freeway and she was hit by a large truck, and she died a few minutes later.

I remember that I was in shock. I could not believe what I was being told, but when they brought a grief counselor in to talk to me it suddenly hit me. Could the legend of the crows be true, I thought. Then I decided that it was nothing more than pure chance that she died shortly after those birds flew through that window. Then I asked, I had to, "Did those birds have anything to do with it?" The counselor had no idea what I was talking about, so I told her what happened. She told me that the story was just an old wives' tale someone had started to make a good story, and that was all it was, then she added that nothing but man's mortality has anything to do with when, where, or how we die.

I could understand what she was saying, but the thought still stayed in my mind, and that thought got stronger when the school started shaking and there was a loud thud that echoed through the hallways.

The fire alarm went off. Now, we had heard that sound more than once since we had monthly fire drills, but this time it was different. The teachers were in the hallway yelling at the students to keep calm and not to run. They always yelled that, but this time their voices were shaky and a little scary. I was rushed out with the others and told to join my class.

"Eighteen, nineteen, twenty," I could hear the teacher saying as he walked among us, counting to make sure how many of us kids were still there. He got to twenty-two and couldn't count anymore. Then, as he finished, he got a panicked look on his face. He counted again and then a third time before he yelled that three of his students were not with the group. Not one other teacher said that they were missing any kids... just my class. Within seconds the principal grabbed some of the teachers and they ran in to search the building.

They searched for about ten minutes before the principal came out and told the teachers to send everyone home for the rest of the week. Considering it was a Monday, we were really happy, but we weren't told what happened... we were just told to leave, and that created more questions, which of course weren't going to be answered. It wasn't until a couple days later that we finally heard what had happened. Three kids, friends of mine unfortunately, were in the restroom and that was where part of the ceiling suddenly collapsed. They said that the children were killed immediately, and didn't feel any pain. Thinking back now, that was a good thing.

Miss Frances' funeral was the next day. The entire town was there and everyone was quiet except for the crying. She had been very much loved by the community and especially by the students she taught. I even liked her which was amazing considering I hated most of the boring old teachers. So I listened to every word the minister said as he praised her contributions to the school and students, but my mind also wandered to the fact that we would have to do this all over again in a few days.

The town hired a large group of grief counselors to come and talk to all of us, but since the school was closed, they visited the students' homes to speak with each of us. My counselor showed up around eight in the evening. I was watching TV when she showed up. I remember that I was fine. Even for a young boy, I knew that everyone was going to die eventually and there was nothing anyone could do about it.

Her name was Nancy Strough. She was nice, but honestly, she treated me like a kid. She explained about birth, life, and death, and then she told me that Miss Frances and my friends were at peace and with The Father, The Son, and The Holy Ghost. "Oh come on," I thought. "They're dead, lady, I know that and you know that, so why are you sugarcoating it?" Now, it wasn't that I wasn't feeling any grief... I was but even I knew that dead was dead and there was no other way to say it. Anyway, I pretended that she was helping, and so by the time she left I was ready for bed.

The next morning I heard that after she left me, Mrs. Strough went a couple houses down to the Sara Jones' house. She knocked on the door and Sara's mother opened it, invited her in and went up to get Sara. All of a sudden she let out a scream. I thought I heard it, but where we lived there were always noises, so I ignored it. Anyway, a couple of minutes later, an ambulance pulled up in front of their house, and a minute after that, they brought a gurney out and placed it in the back.

I could see from my room they had someone on the gurney. Whoever it was small. The entire neighborhood was out watching so, of course, I went out too. It was then that I heard. When Sara's mom went up to get her daughter, she found Sara cuddled up under the blanket. Once she pulled the blanket, she found Sara lying in a pool of blood. It was dried, so Sara must have been dead for a very long time.

The stories started immediately that she had died from coughing too hard and rupturing a vein in the chest, causing her to drown in her own blood. I just laughed when I heard that. I was beginning to believe the legend that the crows and not just circumstance was causing all these deaths.

Honestly, it was getting to where I was spending more time at funerals than I was spending at home. By the end of that week, two more of my classmates had died. Still, although no one could explain why so many out of a single group were dying, no one thought of the crows. Finally, the council held a meeting where anyone who had anything to say about the subject could come and speak.

Through all of the crying and whispering a few of the adults got up and gave reasons why it was happening, but none of them made any sense. At last, an indigenous elder from a nearby settlement stood up.

"This has happened before," he said. "More than two generations ago, it happened in the north of this land. A flight of crows flew into a nursery. They landed one after another on the cribs until not one of them was left untouched. Within a fortnight each of the babies died, some with illness and others through accident. It was not until it was too late that they realized what had happened and learned how to prevent it from happening again."

"And how is that," someone from the audience asked.

"They decided to exterminate every crow within a kilometer of the settlement," he replied. "After all, more than one thousand crows were killed and burned. The crows never returned and there has been no outbreak of deaths that has ever occurred since then."

It didn't take long for the council to decide that our little town had to follow the example of that settlement. It was ordered that a five shillings bounty be paid for the head of each crow that was killed, until there were no crows left in the area.

More than thirty five hundred crows were killed over the next few months. That order has been maintained through all of these years, and every year hundreds of crows are killed and turned in to the council.

Now, all over Australia believe me there are still crows, and no doubt some may even once in a while fly into people's houses, but let me assure you not one single crow will do so in our town. Over the years, the killing of any crow in the area crows has worked. There are no more crows flying in through open school windows, or any sort of window for that matter.

Pity, though, it did not help those children who were cursed and died over the next few days so long ago. I am always grateful, as I was in that classroom that day, a crow never landed on my desk so I was one of the few who has lived to tell the tale. Happily, after that diabolical day, the curse of the crows never again came back to haunt our town, so we now live a fairly normal routine life, except sadly for the memory that continually haunts our dreams of Miss Frances and those twenty innocent children who died so long ago.

The Wreck of the Batavia

By the grace of our most holy God and King William of The Netherlands, I sit here on the shores New Holland as my life is coming to an end, and I have a story to tell, the truth about the shipwreck on her maiden voyage, of the flagship of The East India Company "The Batavia".

My name is Aad Ostrander… well that isn't really important, as I was simply a member of the crew who worked below deck, maintaining the supply of food and fresh water for the entire ship's crew. The ships Commander was Francisco Pelsaert and our skipper Adriaen Jacobsz.

As on all ocean voyages, the going was under extreme and difficult conditions, and it was my duty to protect the crew and officers from scurvy and malnutrition, not an easy task I can assure you. Actually, we were luckier than most, as the commander made it a point to stop in ports along our journey to resupply and give the men some time off the ship. Even so tensions on board were high; we had a lot of trouble makers aboard led by Jeronimus Cornelisz, a zealot Mennonite and an apothecary and under merchant who was in charge of the ship's cargo.

I personally hated the man, he treated me like a dog, but there was nothing I could do, he was very friendly with our skipper, Adriaen Jacobsz, who we all knew resented the fact that The East India Company had appointed a merchant in command of the flagship. It was obvious to any fool that there was great tension between Pelsaert and our Captain, it was rumored they had also voyaged together on a previous ship.

As ours was the flagship we were also carrying a king's ransom of gold, silver, and jewels. Knowing all this, it was rumored below decks that Cornelisz and Captain Jacobsz were planning a mutiny against the Commander. Their plans were to take the treasure and the ship, and after that make their way to the nearest mainland to start a new life with all they had taken. Their evil plan suddenly altered when land was sighted where no commander or sailor expected it to be.

Immediately, Cornelisz started spreading the rumor that food and water were low, he insisted that if we did not make landfall soon we would be in serious trouble. I knew better, but not one person, especially the captain listened to me. So, despite the fact we had supplies for at least another ten, maybe twelve days, the decision was made to stop and gather some fruits and fresh water on the approaching group of small islands.

Despite the fact that the sails were lowered, the ship drifted for quite a time. The thing was, I swear, I never once heard the lookout warn of any danger in the water until the last second, and then I heard yelling louder than I had ever heard it before. Someone had spotted shallow water ahead and the ship was heading directly toward it.

Now, I had not been at sea as long as the men who served up on the deck, but even I could tell that the ship was moving strangely. The waves were lifting the bow way out of the water and then dropping it back down with a thud. It was not until I heard sounds from the bottom of the hull and saw water flowing between the planks that I knew what it was. It was not a sandbar... a sandbar would not do that kind of damage or make the kind of sounds I was hearing. We had landed on rocks or maybe possibly even a reef, but whatever it was the ship was too damaged to make it any further.

We sat there overnight in silence, not going anywhere. It was scary, usually there were always sounds on a ship, but on this disastrous night it was deathly quiet, then at dawn the cry "Abandon ship," was shouted from the bridge and was echoed throughout the crew. The crew rushed below deck and grabbed everything they could and either loaded it into boats, or simply threw it into the water to be retrieved by the men swimming alongside.

There has always been a superstition that women should never be on a sailing ship, as even just one woman aboard would cause disaster to befall any ship and crew carrying them.

Out of the 322 people aboard the Batavia there were a number of women and children, so unfortunately a lot of the crew was now blaming them for the accident. Me, I never believed that legend so, once I got up on deck, I helped as many women and children as I could get safely ashore.

Between the sharks, the current and mere exhaustion, we the survivors watched in horror as forty people disappeared under the waves... never to be seen again. The rest of us, praise the Lord... we made it to shore, but for those forty who did not make, we didn't realize it at the time, but they were actually the lucky ones.

The island we landed on was desolate with few trees, very little green grass and no animals that we were able to detect, other than seabirds and, as always, rats. Rats everywhere, we were it seemed cursed, but as this desolate place looked like it was going to be our home for a very long time, we set out to make it as secure as we could.

The moment we abandoned ship, we knew how bad our situation was, as we watched the Batavia sink below the waves, a number of fins rose from the bloodstained water. Other than that... there was nothing to see.

Once ashore some of the crew felt betrayed and seethed with anger when Commander Francisco Pelsaert, Skipper Adriaen Jacobsz and a group of others decided that they would take the two long boats and head off to the mainland to find water, if unable to do that, they would then head back to Batavia.

So we were stuck in this hellish place, and eventually, when our meager supplies ran out, we apparently would all just left on the God forsaken land to starve. Even I knew that if the Commander and Captain did make it back to Batavia, the trip there and back to rescue us would take months.

To make matters worse, they had stocked their boat with a large amount of the remaining water and supplies. That left us with nothing to really eat. We survived a while on the paltry supplies left us, but as these supplies got shorter, rationing was imposed and, after a while, even those became less and less. Yeah, some of the men did try to fish, we also cooked some of the sparse vegetation on the island, but it was not nearly enough for so many people.

Although we had built what you could call a community, even so things were not peaceful. Every hour, tensions built between the few remaining petty officers, and Jeronimus Cornelisz and his followers. The officers tried to keep control, but there was no way that was going to happen. Soon, these islands that had offered us sanctuary were turning, slowly, into a living hell.

As the under merchant, Cornelisz was in charge, with a plan to get rid of all official authority, he sent the officers headed by Wiebbe Hayes to another Island to search for water. Once they were gone, this sadistic psychotic killer set about convincing his followers that, to survive, they would have to kill all the other remaining survivors. So the first thing he did was to order his group of about 20 men to trash the rest of the longboats. He said that he didn't want anyone else to leave the island. He didn't say why... he just wanted it that way, and that was the way it was going to be.

Day after day he and his men killed people... sometimes sadistically one at a time, but more often there were two or three killed. It didn't matter to him. The men they set about killing first... then the children were next, and lastly the women. The women were kept 'til last as they were used for sex and other perversions. It was a very gruesome sight to see Cornelisz and his men use their swords to run the person through, and then cut them open from their pelvis to their chests, and then he would laugh as they fell to the ground and bled to death. He didn't even bother burying most of them... they were left in the weeds and sun to rot. The stench was unbelievable.

As the people were slaughtered, I was ordered to "supply" his followers with food from the now rather plentiful source available. Honestly, I swear on the Lord Jesus, I more than hated what I had to do, I had nightmares about it every night, but I knew that if I didn't do as they told me to do... I would be the next to be killed and devoured.

Within two months the situation went from bad to worse, and people started realizing that help wasn't coming. It got to the point where suicide, became an easy thought to have, after all the ocean was just at our doorstep, and between the waves and the distance, it would have made it easy just to swim out and not come back. A few people did exactly that, but not that many.

Some of the people built makeshift forts out of rocks and sticks from the shoreline. They did all they could to escape being Cornelisz next victim. The forts alas, did not work; Cornelisz's men just immediately massacred anyone who was hiding there.

In the end, along with five women, I was the only male left on Beacon Island who wasn't one of Cornelisz's murderers. The reason I wasn't killed was that they needed me to butcher the few bodies left that they thought suitable to eat, but I knew that eventually... I would be killed and eaten the same as the others.

Before that happened, thank the Lord, the Commander returned with a ship full of soldiers, and soon learned from one of the remaining women all the gruesome things that had been happening on Beacon, and immediately Commander Francisco Pelsaert captured Cornelisz and his men. Some were taken back for trial to Batavia, but Cornelisz and several others were headed for a different fate. I was relieved, also, that any remaining bodies found on the Island were given a true Christian burial.

Me, I was scared stiff... just me being alive implicated me as one of the murderers, so I had hidden at the first signs of the rescuers approached the island. I learnt later that Cornelisz and several others of his men had both their hands cut off and were executed on Seal Island. This made me realize I had been right hiding; I was the butcher, who had prepared the dead human bodies for consumption by those evil bastards. Nothing I said could ever excuse that, it would have been said that I should have allowed them to kill me, rather than do what I did. So with all this in mind, I hid till they had all gone, and then I set about surviving on that God forgotten Island.

From time to time, fishermen stopped to shelter from pending storms, and once even Pirates. These Pirates soon found they had a pregnant whore from the Spice Islands on board, so rather than kill her, they dumped her on a nearby Island and left. I could hear her screams across the water. By that time I had made myself a raft for fishing, it was how I had learnt to survive, to tell the truth, I had come to like my way of life on those God forsaken shores. Yet I was lonely, I had not set eyes on a woman in years, desire and curiosity got the better of me. So I set off to save the whore.

Aku made a good companion, I'll admit she was not much to look at, but beside the child she was pregnant with, she also bore me a son and survived with me and tried to be the best companion she could. To tell the truth, eventually I actually cared about her more than I could say.

Four years later, due to my failing health, we were taken by an Asian fishing vessel to New Holland.

There are times now that I actually miss Beacon Island, this bloody country is rough going, between the soldiers, convicts, free settlers, black natives, crocs, flies and the floods and droughts, it's a bugger of a life. I pray the Lord my sons will survive and make a good life for themselves. Maybe one day out of curiosity they may even sail away to the city of my birth Antwerp.

It has now been about ten years since the sinking of the Batavia. I still wake up at times in a cold sweat; sadly, due to all that took place there on that desolate island, my health has been greatly suffered. I now have only a few weeks to live and I will never see my sons grown and settled, so I want the true story of all that happened under the dastardly hands of Cornelisz and his men to be known. As my word to God this is my dying declaration and I swear that every word of it is true and honest. Now, I can die with my sons knowing that I die here in New Holland with an untarnished soul, and yet a tortured heart. May God Forgive me for my sins.

Signed --- Aad Ostrander

The Bunyip's Lesson

If you are walking past any waterway in Australia, especially in the South East, it is not the crocodiles that you have to worry about. It is an enormous creature called a Bunyip. Although descriptions vary according to where you are, it is common to hear that they are a tremendous ugly beast with, some say, fangs, flippers, and a horse-like tail. The worst thing about these animals is that they come out at night to feed, and their meals have been known to include humans if disturbed.

Bunyips are known to Aboriginals as a "punishing" creature, but today's media has hidden the truth about what these creatures are capable of. Unfortunately, Honour King found out just how punishing they could be.

Honour was just eighteen when she was out driving. It wasn't in the real Aussie Outback, but it could have been. It was miles and miles of nothing except a few stands of gum trees in the middle of endless farmers' fields. She was a good student, earning straight A's and making honor roll every year. She had an attention span that would make most people cry if they knew how long it was. But that night, the endless sound of the tires, the vast empty spaces, the lack of a radio station, and her female hormones running rampant caused her mind to wander to the hot boy who was in her geometry class.

It was at that moment, about two kilometers down the road, that a koala climbed down from a small gum tree and started walking toward the road. One did not know why, but the animal stopped at the edge of the road. Maybe it saw something that interested it, maybe it was just tired, but it stopped just for a minute before stepping out into the road.

Honour wasn't really paying attention to her driving as she sped down the road. She covered the two kilometers in less than two minutes and didn't see the koala on the road. All she felt was the thump and the car jump when she ran over its body. "What was that?" she asked, as her mind went back to her driving. Then, as she continued down the road, her thoughts were never on the bump she had felt; instead, all she was thinking about was that hot-looking boy in her class... If she had been paying attention to the bump, she would undoubtedly have stopped, and when she found out she had hit a koala, she would have tried her best to save its life. She adored the furry little creatures and would always have done everything she could to save it.

She also never knew that it was a female koala with a very young Joey in its pouch, and that the two of them would die soon after she hit them. If she had known what she had killed, she would have been devastated.

However, a young Bunyip was up in the tree when the koala had climbed down and started to cross the road, and it saw everything. As soon as the car passed by, he ran over to the dying koala. He looked into its eyes and saw into its soul. The Bunyip knew its friend was dying, and so was its baby. All it could do was comfort the dying animal.

It was well known that, a long time ago in Aboriginal legends, a Bunyip and a koala had been friends. Once again, against all rules of the bush, this young Bunyip had also formed a friendship with this particular mother and her Joey, even though the mother koala knew this was frowned on by the majority of koalas, as they had no desire to displease the entire koala community.

Unfortunately, the koala and her joey did not survive. In the second, the koala died, the Bunyip raised its head and screamed as if it was telling heaven to welcome this mother and baby. Then the Bunyip's feelings changed as it became enraged at the loss of its friend and the indifference of this fiendish human, who had not even stopped to see what it had done.

The young Bunyip's claws came out, and it began hissing and growling, and its eyes became a bright flaming red as it watched the car as it drove off. Suddenly, the Bunyip started to running down the road at such a speed that it soon gained on the vehicle, but as he did, he began to slow down and decided instead to follow at a distance as he made a vow that this young human was going to indeed suffer for the koala's and her Joey's death.

Honour pulled into her family's driveway about 20 minutes later. She got out and went straight inside the house, not even bothering to look at the car to see if it was damaged or, even worse, if any animal was stuck on her bumper. If she had looked, she would have seen on the bumper a lot of fresh and dried blood and a crack in the car's plastic covering.

The young Bunyip ran into the driveway just a moment later. Its fury had not faded in the least; in fact, it had become a lot more intense... especially when it observed the fresh blood splatters on the car. Then, the Bunyip did something that no one ever heard of a Bunyip doing... it licked at the blood, and as it tasted it, a deep guttural growl started in its chest and explosively left its mouth, shattering a small glass window in the garage.

On hearing the terrible howls, Honour's dad grabbed his cricket bat in the hall and ran out the front door. He knew that the sound had to have come from an animal, and he thought that if an animal sounded like that, it had to be big and most likely dangerous, but once he got into the driveway, there was nothing to be seen. He walked back into the house and yelled out to everyone that everything was okay, it was probably a large, wounded stray dog.

Honour went upstairs to her room. After changing her clothes, she spoke with a friend on her mobile for a while and then sat on the edge of her bed, reading.

The Bunyip stood on an old tree stump, watching the house intently. He saw the lights go on in Honour's room. Climbing up an old gum tree, he was able to watch Honour get undressed, and he saw her with her back to the window. Silently, he climbed down the tree, and then with his sharp, big claws, he began climbing up the side of the house until he was at her window. He tried to observe what he could about this monster that had coldly killed his friend, then he saw something that he could use... to let her know she had been observed killing the koala and Joey. The female human had a stuffed bear lying on her bed... right next to her pillow. To get the girls' attention, the Bunyip scraped its claws down the glass. It was loud, and it sounded like a hundred pieces of chalk scratching across a blackboard.

Not disturbed by the sound at first Honour muttered to herself out loud as she kept on reading "I wish my dad would cut that branch off... the noise it makes hitting the window is so annoying," suddenly she stopped reading as she got an uneasy feeling that something was looking at her, she knew she was all alone upstairs and she could hear her parents watching TV, so it certainly was not them. She initially brushed off this feeling, but it persisted, so she stood up and looked towards the window, where she saw a creature unlike anything she had ever seen.

She stood there absolutely terrified. It was enormous, covered in fur, its bared teeth would have been able to chew through anything, and its massive furrowed brow emphasized its anger. Suddenly, it growled very softly, but the sound sent shivers through Honour's spine. It was utterly terrifying and very guttural, and the look in its eyes sent shudders through Honour's body as she screamed in shock. Hearing her scream, the creature gave a loud, piercing growl as it bared its teeth at Honour menacingly, then this large, horrifying, insane creature dropped to the ground and disappeared into the night.

    The petrified Honour couldn't stop shaking as she ran downstairs and headed straight into her mother's arms. She was screaming just as if she had just seen a ghost or a dead body for the first time. Her concerned parents asked her what was wrong, but she was too shaken to tell them. She sat in her dad's chair, crying and shaking. Eventually, after her mother gave her a calming sedative, she fell asleep. Before she had a chance to tell them what had happened, her dad carried his daughter back to her bedroom and turned out the light. The Bunyip saw the light go out, and he climbed back up to the window and stayed there all night watching this killer human.

    Honour didn't wake up until quite late in the morning. Her parents had already left for work, so she hurriedly started to get ready for school. She would be late, but they had a special project just after lunch, and she did not want to miss it. As she dressed, she began to wonder if what she had seen at the window was real, or if she had merely been having a bad dream. After all, monsters like that did not just exist.

    She closed her bedroom door and took a quick shower. Strangely, the bedroom door was open when she came back, and the moment she walked back in the room, she saw that the glass from her window was piled in shards on the floor. Then she noticed that her pillow was stained. It was dark red, nearly brown. She walked over. She was sure that it was blood, and once again, the terrible fear she had felt the night before returned. "Where did that come from?" she cried out. Taking the pillow in her hand, she saw her stuffed bear, which she treasured, sitting on the floor at the foot of her bed. It was torn to shreds and covered with blood. There were muddy animal footprints leading to the window, but when she looked, there was no one or nothing there. She was now absolutely terrified.

As her parents had already left for work, all she could do was get dressed and head to school. She was absolutely frightened, and at that moment, school seemed to her the safest place.

She dressed quickly, rushed downstairs, and into the living room, where she picked up her backpack. As she walked out of the room, she saw hiding in the shadows the same terrifying, enormous creature she had seen at her bedroom window, and the eyes were the same angry, menacing eyes she had seen the night before..

"What do you want?" Honour cried out in utter fear. The weird, enormous creature just stood there watching every move she made. She could hear it making noises. They were not growling noises exactly, they were shrill, piercing sounds, but at least it wasn't quite as horrifying as the noise she had heard the night before. She slowly made her way towards the front door. Her eyes were locked on it, and the creature's eyes were locked on her. "What do you want?" she cried out again, but this time it was not her normal voice... she was yelling in sheer panic.

The Bunyip's claws reached out and dug into the back of the couch. They cut deep gouges into the black leather, over and over again; they dug in, ripping the couch apart. Honour was truly terrified for her life. She screamed as the enormous creature moved towards her and sprang into the air. It missed her chest by inches, as once again it gave out the most hideous, frightening growl, then it turned and ran out of the room into the kitchen, and then out the back door. Honour could hear the screen door bang as this monster let out one final piercing howl.

Needless to say, by now Honour was utterly panicked; she was shaking so hard she could not even use her mobile phone. When she did, she found she had forgotten to recharge it, and the charger she had left in her dad's car. She was far too scared to leave the house and head to school; she knew only too well that the creature was out there waiting. So she quickly locked every door and window, even the inside doors. She tried to use their house phone, but the wires had been cut. She then once again heard the monster pounding on the back door; all she could do was to hide in the bathroom, as it had no windows, with a large kitchen knife by her side, waiting for the monster to pounce and kill her, or for her mom and dad to come home.

Eventually, the pounding on the door stopped, but she could still hear the hideous growling. It went on for hours, and then suddenly all was silent. The dead silence was even more frightening.

When she did, after what seemed like a lifetime, hear her father's car in the driveway, she immediately rushed out of the bathroom seeking comfort and protection, but her father didn't even give her a chance to say a word. "Honour," he yelled as he walked into the house, "Honour, come here immediately, I want to know what you damn well hit with my car?"

Of course, she did not know what she had done, so she denied hitting anything other than a bump in the road. "That's bullshit, Honour! There is a lot of blood on the front of my car, and I want to know where it came from, and I want to know why the car is damaged, and I want to know RIGHT NOW!" Again, she denied hitting anything, so he grabbed her by the arm, led her out the door, and angrily pushed his protesting daughter into the car.

"Take me where you hit that bump," he said angrily, with a deep, hidden concern that his daughter may have hit something besides a bump in the road. Honor burst into tears and tried to tell her dad about the monster, but he wouldn't listen. He truly believed she was making up this story to protect herself from punishment over the damage to his car. Crying softly and still shaking, she directed him along the route she had taken. They drove for about 20 kilometres before she told him to stop.

"It was right here," she said as she stepped out of the car.

"I don't see any bumps," her dad said as he walked around the front of the car. Suddenly, what he saw was a dead koala lying on the side of the road. He looked at her with disgust. "You didn't even stop, did you!" he stated furiously. He was angrier than he had ever been. Then he saw Joey's body lying on the ground next to his mother. "You killed a baby, too. How could you not have at least stopped?"

Honour stood there, the tears pouring down her face, she didn't... couldn't... say a word, and she was so upset and ashamed at what she had done without even knowing it

Suddenly, her dad saw something standing a little bit up the road. He could not make out what kind of animal it was; to him, it looked like some kangaroo. He did not know it, as his eyesight was not so good, but it was the young Bunyip that had been frightening his daughter. "Honour, come here," he ordered. "What has been happening is that creature up the road, like the monster you have been telling me about?"

The Bunyip moved off the road and drove down towards them, climbing a nearby tree so he could hear better. Honour burst into hysterical tears and once again began to explain everything in detail, recounting how terrified she had been.

Her father sympathized with his daughter about her terrifying day, but he did not really believe a word of it; possibly, he thought a stray wild dog may have wandered into the house. Wild dog or not, at present, he was dealing with a dead koala, and he felt his daughter should have done the responsible thing and stopped when she felt that bump on a flat surface.

He looked at her sternly and said. "You are not a responsible driver, Honour. As a punishment, I want your keys and your license right now."

She gave him the keys, and he then took the keys and threw them as far as he could into the bush. Then he also took his cigarette lighter out of his pocket, asked for her driver's license, and burned it right in front of her. "Also, my gal, no more Internet for a month and no parties whatsoever".

The Bunyip heard every word and growled, but it was not a mean growl. It was observed that this young human was being severely punished, so his friend's tragic death was now not going unnoticed. He also felt some relief that, as her father was dealing with it, he would no longer have to seek further revenge.

Honour's father took a shovel out of his boot, picked up the koala and her Joey, and carefully buried them under a tree, a reasonable distance from the road. The Bunyip was crying softly as his friends' bodies were laid in the ground. He did not interfere; he just watched with relief.

As a last punishment Honour's Dad got in the car, locked the doors and started driving away. Honour ran to the car, crying, and asked him what he was doing. "You need to learn a lesson," he said. "Home is that way." He pointed back toward town. "But what about that monster?" she cried, "There are no such things as monsters, Honour, you are exaggerating to cover up for what you have done. I'll see you in my study when you WALK home."

Honour was genuinely terrified, but she did not walk home; instead, she ran all the way. The young Bunyip followed her, but did not reveal himself; it looked like she was being punished enough. Eventually, he turned around, gave out one loud, piercing growl, and headed back into the bush.

Oh yes, Honour was suitably punished; it was years before she ever drove a car again or even walked alone in the bush. The koala and her baby got a respectable funeral, so the Bunyip was satisfied that justice had been done, and everything in the universe was once again set right...

The Call of the Raven

It was not a typical night. Yes, the sun had set in the west, over the Victoria Central Highlands, but there was something different about the night the small settlement in the Ballarat region was going to face. Even though the day had been cloudy and rainy, as soon as the light died, the clouds parted, and the rain, which had puddled on the ground, returned to the skies, and the air cleared so that looking at the stars was like looking into the Lord's perfect diamond.

There was no moon that night, but some swore on their Bibles that they could see a faint mist of red surrounding where the moon should have been. Many, including the local priests, said that it was a bad omen. They called it a Blood Moon, but that night it was different... so different.

The birds and animals were strangely missing or quiet that night. Even pet dogs were nowhere to be seen. The night birds who usually made such a din that some found it hard to sleep were deathly still that evening. It was most disconcerting to some of the older residents, who had heard their song for generation upon generation. One 75-year-old man said that it was the first time in his many years that he had heard such silence from the forest. The silence, though, did not translate over to the people of the town.

Most were in the square that night. They weren't celebrating anything in particular, they were in the town's two pubs just drinking. When the pubs finally closed, they all gathered in the town square, singing, dancing, and enjoying themselves, filled with life and living. Even the youngest children were allowed to stay awake until the wee hours of the night, and more than a few got their first sips of ale from their fathers, uncles, and older brothers. It is said that a couple of children, under the influence, painted slogans on the town's main building. There was no proof of this, but it made a nice story since no one else would ever take credit for the pranks that night.

In the morning, the bodies of the intoxicated lined the square. A few of the slightly stronger spirits were walking on unsteady legs as they tried to find their way home or, in most cases, trying to find their clothes and relatives lost the night before. The children, who had for the most part remained sober, ran around the square yelling and banging pots and pans, much to the dismay of the adults.

Unnoticed, the birds and animals were still absent save one. A raven, black as the coal they used in their fires and as large as a good-sized turkey, sat on the church's cross. It was silent as it looked down on the square. If anyone had been able to look into its eyes, they would have recognized a disdain for the town and its people, as well as all that was taking place.

A young man of no more than 13 looked up and saw the bird. "Look," he yelled, "Look up at the church's cross." Everyone stopped and looked up, and as they did, the raven let out a screech that was unlike anything anyone in the square had ever heard before. "What does it want?"

"I do not know," the priest answered. "Some would say that a raven that is pure of blackness is a bad omen. It is said that a family or even an entire town can be cursed by just its appearance. The one consolation is that a raven will never harm a young child."

Just then, the raven let out another hideous scream as he flew down and landed on a statue in the center of the square. Some tried to scare the bird off, but they were greeted with violent movements and demonic hisses. Some of the children threw rocks, but the bird caught the closest one in its beak and threw it to the ground.

While everyone looked at the bird, a young woman asked a question. "But Father, doesn't the raven live on the islands four days' travel south of here? They never come this far north. Surely, we have crows and ibis, but ravens... There has never been one in our town before."

Another voice came from the crowd. "Maybe God sent it to us," it asked. "Maybe it is not a curse at all; maybe it is the sign of a forthcoming miracle?" Not one other person said a word or uttered a question. They were all, for once, silent.

Suddenly, without warning, the raven let loose with the loudest scream, as it opened its massive wings and launched itself from the statue. It circled the square not just once or twice, but three times before it silently glided between two buildings and out of sight. However, the echoes of its final scream lasted for what seemed to be an eternity before it also left through many passages out of the town.

The people were perplexed, and some felt uneasy, not understanding the meaning of the raven's appearance or the strange noises it had made. Some even panicked and quickly scrambled back to their shops or homes. Others stood and just talked, trying to find meaning in what had happened, some even worrying if the appearance of the raven was a warning of the downfall of the town.

The children, the most innocent of all, played on the cobblestone plaza, all quite unaware of anything special happening. To them, it was just another day, and the raven was just another bird... loud, but just another bird all the same.

During the next few hours, the raven circled the square an uncountable number of times. Each time it did, the image of the bird invoked feelings of fear and dread as well as others of wonder and curiosity. Finally, as the sun began to set on the mountains, the raven landed on the steps outside the church. Looking proud and brave, it walked back and forth on the steps, surveying the growing crowd of people.

An old man, one of the town's older residents and a popular choirmaster at the church, walked to the steps and sat down, watching the raven the whole time. "What are you doing here?" he asked as the bird walked closer to him. "Are you a messenger from God or a demon sent to us by Satan?" Of course, it was rhetorical, but nevertheless, he asked.

The raven launched himself from the steps, circled the square, looking at the people who had assembled below, and landed on the old man's knee.

"I am neither from God, nor from Satan," the raven said as he looked into the old man's eyes. "I am here to give you a sad message, but it comes from me and not one of your self-designed deities."

The old man and the assembled people gazed in awe at what they considered a miracle. Not one person said a word. Most were too scared to even move... afraid that they might offend the bird that actually spoke and that had come among them.

"I bring dire news to you," the raven said.

"What is that," the old man asked, expecting to hear that there was going to be a disaster that would affect everyone in the town or maybe the bird was a forecast of death. The crowd was gathering, all intently listening to the Raven. Some were very frightened, not understanding, but all were too amazed to walk away.

"Last night during your celebration there was a moment of great sadness," the raven replied. "You did not know about it, but I am sure that some of you felt it in your hearts."

The gathered people looked around. No one said anything, but there was a look among a few of them. It was as if they knew what the raven spoke of.

"Two of your young died last night at the far end of the gorge," the raven continued. "It was a male and a female of different races and different cultures. They threw themselves from a ledge, landing on sharp rocks beneath. They suffered greatly, and their bodies are still untouched. I know this because I was there and watched their death. It was not pleasant to watch and less pleasant to tell you of."

The people looked around. A few dashed to their homes to search for their teenage children, who were not among the crowd. Within minutes, a scream of grief and then another was heard echoing through the square.

"They who lost their loved ones now realize their loss," the raven said. "The young ones were very much in love, but were forbidden to consummate their love because of their differences, and that was what caused their death. Nothing else could have. They were meant for each other, but hatred, envy, and sheer bigotry tried to murder their love and instead stole their lives."

"What do you mean?" the old man asked.

"Ask the council," the raven replied as he spread his wings and lifted into the air. "Ask the council!" The bird circled the square, repeating the words, "ask the council" over and over again until his voice was drowned out by the sobbing of the parents who had lost their loved ones.

"Who was it? Who were those young people?" the old man asked.

One of the town council members stepped forward. He was James Pankert. He was one of the founders of the town, and it was said that he was not a day less than 105 years old. No one knew if it was true, or not, but then again, no one questioned what was said by Pankert or any of the other council members in this small community; their word was law.

"The two who died are Annie Welsh and Joshua Long," he said. "They asked my permission to marry weeks ago. They told me that they had been in love since they were young children playing in a sandbox, but they knew, because of their backgrounds and the intense bigotry in the town, that they would not be allowed to marry. I told them that the town would approve their marriage; however, I said that I must consult with their respective families first.

Both fathers were angry because the young people had gone to me without asking their permission; they also said they would never condone it under any circumstances. So the fathers ordered that their children be sent to separate, distant townships as a punishment.

   So, they came to me again and told me that they had decided to run away together and marry in the next town. Still, apparently, they were so scared of their families' wrath, so instead of that, they must have decided to end their lives and be together with God and the angels in heaven. That was apparently the only thing they believed they could do, so they would not be separated, and be together for eternity."

   Upon learning of the tragic love story, the town began a long mourning period, as the young men of the town walked the many miles to where the raven told them to go. At the base of one of the many sheer cliffs, they found the bodies. Annie was dressed in a white dress, symbolizing her innocence, while Joshua wore the colors of his family. The bodies were close together as if they fell together, and one thing the searchers noticed… The couple's hands were intertwined, and they were holding a pair of gold bands… The rings they were going to use to become husband and wife.

   It took the searchers many hours to get back to town, and when they did, it was a moment of intense mourning and a moment of great decision.

   The town council met with the parents. The discussions lasted through the night and well into the morning. Finally, they emerged with a decision. Pankert and the town leaders stood behind the parents, who were strangely silent.

   "Annie and Joshua died because of our stupidity," Pankert said. "They came for help and were turned away, left to the judgment of parents who did not realize the true feelings of their children. It has been decided that the two young people shall be married as of this moment, and they shall be buried together, holding hands and wearing the rings they carried. This is our decision, and it is beyond contestation.

In the future, parents must learn to understand their children's feelings and not ignore them, but respect them instead. Our children must never be afraid to come to us and talk without retribution. It is our word that a tragedy such as this will never happen again."

That afternoon, Annie and Joshua were buried together, holding hands and wearing the rings that they died with. Tears were shed by family, friends, and town leaders, but there was also a sense of celebration. A new age of openness spread across the town. Young people spoke with their parents, many of whom were married, and others lived new and happy lives. Because of the sacrifice of two young people, there has never been another couple whose lives were destroyed due to ignorance.

And the raven, it never returned to the town. It had delivered its message and was no longer needed. And that was the real blessing.

The Great Emu War Of 1932

Australia had such a valiant history. Fighting at Gallipoli and all over Europe in WWI. So when 1932 came around, the Australian military was very proud of itself, its men, and all that it had done. Then came the war that Australia thought would be a walk in the park, but it turned out to be far more.

It was that year when troops were sent to Campion in Western Australia to fight the most dangerous enemy Australia ever faced...50 Emus!

Residents of the area, including ex-soldiers, were sent to Canberra (Australia's capital) to ask for help since the number of Emus had increased to more than 20,000, who had come to mate, breed, and eat. Sadly, they also destroyed the fence, which allowed wild rabbits to flood the area and eat all the crops.

Beyond belief, Canberra, mainly Minister of Defence, Sir George Pearce, ordered a group of ex-military to fight the war and even supplied them with machine guns and bullets (a rare thing for an army to have). They were sent to the area. All being ex-military, they knew how deadly machine guns could be. Then the war started.

On November 2, 1932, the military travelled to Campion, under the command of Major Meredith, where some 50 emus had been sighted. The birds were out of range of the guns, so the locals attempted to herd the emus into an area where they could be ambushed. However, the birds split into small groups and ran, making them challenging targets. The first series of shots fired was ineffective due to the distance between the Emus. A second round of gunfire was able to kill "a number" of birds. Later the same day, a small flock was encountered, and "perhaps a dozen" birds were killed.

    On the 4th of November, Major Meredith had prepared for an ambush near a local dam, and over 1,000 emus were spotted heading towards their position. This time they waited until the birds were at point-blank range before opening fire. The gun jammed after only 12 birds were killed, and the remaining emus scattered before more could be killed.

In the days that followed, Major Meredith chose to move further south, where the birds were "reported to be fairly tame". By the 8th of November, only 6 days into the war, 2,500 rounds of ammunition had been fired. Considering so many shots were fired, the emu casualties were not great. The number of birds killed is unclear: one account claims just 50 birds, but other accounts range from 200 to 500.

Fortunately for Major Meredith, the military had not suffered any casualties at the hands of the Emus, according to his official report anyway.

By the sixth day of the war, the Emu Command had begun to use new techniques...gorilla techniques...to defeat their enemy. They ordered their large army to break into smaller groups, which made the Australian armament almost useless. One Emu general was heard saying," We know this land, and we know that these farmers are just people who couldn't make it in the city. So, we will use our wits and our smarts, and we will kick their butts all the way back to Brisbane." The cheer from his soldiers could be heard at least ten miles away.

Following the continuous negative and humorous press coverage, Sir George Pearce ordered a full-on retreat. A few days after that, the Australian Parliament voted to cancel the war and, jokingly, issue the Emus all Medals of Valour for the way they fought and defended themselves from attacks from the Australian military.

A short time later, the Emus returned, and the farmers requested that the Australian military come to their aid. This time, after such a severe defeat the first time, the representatives from the government ignored all rules of politeness and said 'no' before shutting their door. However, the farmers did receive a large number of guns and a plentiful supply of bullets, and they did what the army could not do...THEY WON THE EMU WAR PART 2, wiping out more than 20,000 emus

After the conflict, Major Meredith said, "If we had a military division with the bullet-carrying capacity of these birds, it would face any army in the world. They can face a machine gun with the invulnerability of tanks. They are like Zulus, whom even dum-dum bullets could not stop."

The Real "Great Emu War" (1932)
- Location: Campion district, Western Australia
- Cause: Around 20,000 emus migrated into farmland, trampling crops and breaking fences, which worsened a rabbit infestation.
- Response: Minister of Defence Sir George Pearce approved a military operation using soldiers and Lewis machine guns to cull the emus.
- Commander: Major G.P.W. Meredith of the Royal Australian Artillery led the operation.
- Outcome:

- Over 2,500 rounds fired.
- Only around 986 emus have been confirmed killed.
- The emus proved elusive, fast, and surprisingly tactical.
- The operation was mocked in the press and eventually abandoned.

Journey To The Black Mountain

I love traveling. My hometown of Allegheny Heights has got to be the most boring place on the planet, at least to me. So, about ten years ago, I moved to Cairns in Australia. I had fallen in love with a hot Aussie Sheila. A couple of years later, when we split up, my adventurous nature moved me to Cooktown. I had first gone there for a couple of weeks, as I had heard about a mysterious place outside of Cooktown. It is said to be one of the most paranormal places on the planet, second only to the Bermuda Triangle, and some claim it may even surpass it.

I liked Cooktown; it was so different from anything I had experienced. So, I went back to Cairns, packed my stuff, and headed back to Cooktown. My kind of place, rough and tough, kinda like the old American West. I liked the remoteness and the "she'll be right, mate" attitude, away from Cairns' hustle and bustle

There is one place in particular, about five miles from town, called Black Mountain. It was called Black Mountain because, despite being in an area that received a lot of sun, the mountain itself was always shrouded in shadow. However, the sides of the mountain weren't the only shadows. The canopy of the trees at the base of the mountain is well overgrown to the extent that walking on the ground around Black Mountain is like walking through an open field at midnight during a new moon. No light at all, except for the flashlight most people carried when they traversed into the area. The darkness must have made the region the perfect place to commit suicide, as apparently there had been quite a few suicides on Black Mountain in the last twenty years, and a lot of missing people, who, it is said, went in there but never came out again.

The strange thing was, some of the bodies of the suicide victims were found lying on the ground... very weird, to say the least, for a body to be found on the ground with the ropes they had hung themselves with still hanging from the tree branches. It was rumored that many may have changed their minds once the rope tightened, or that their deaths were due to foul play. Also, all the bodies found looked as if they had been mummified or, as one investigator stated, dehydrated by radiation, but then the question was asked, radiation from what? The scariest thing, though, was the fact that some dehydrated bodies found were dead less than a week.

Some people claimed to have seen lights floating around Black Mountain, but no one, not even the most ardent advocate, had taken a picture of any light, orb, or even a flying saucer. Additionally, not one of the "official" citizens of Cooktown has reported seeing any lights or strange phenomena. Yet there are those visiting the area who will argue till the cows come home that they have seen them, and no amount of proof to the contrary will even convince them otherwise.

Well, anyway, let's get back to the story. One morning back a couple of years ago, a group of kids and I were walking close to the Black Mountain forest, but not in it, as let me tell you, there is not a parent within a hundred miles who would ever give their permission for their child to go anywhere near the actual mountain. Its reputation is far too sinister, so many have entered and never returned.

Anyway, whilst we were walking, one of the girls looked across at one of the trees and observed that there was a note nailed to the bark. It read, "I must end this agony tonight. Do not try to find me because I do not want to be found. I cannot live any longer without my Arthur. I have waited patiently for so long, but I now know the Black Mountain has taken him from me forever." The note also gave a time of 12:35 PM. There was no date or other information... just the note and the time. But the letter wasn't weather-beaten, as one would suspect from an older note. However, who was to know when it was written? It was a note not to be ignored. If it were recent, then maybe a woman's life could be saved.

We didn't waste any time. I grabbed the note... you know, come to think of it now, we could have considered that note a grave marker. Still, at the time I wasn't thinking with a clear mind, as it was already quite late. I wanted to get those youngsters back to town before lunch, as promised, to their parents. So, as I said, I grabbed the note, rushed back to the car, and got those kids safely to their homes before heading into town and straight to the police station.

Now, I was well known at the police station. Since I became a resident of Cooktown, I did a lot of exploring around the town and found a variety of items that I turned in to the police until the rightful owners could be found, cameras, walking sticks, sunglasses, and even an old wallet containing $ 200.

Anyway, I took the note the kids and I had found and handed it over to the guy in charge. Once the officers read the note, they seemed as confused about it as I was. I told them that there was nothing else anywhere in their sight except that note. They immediately called the local hotels and motels but they weren't missing anyone and the state had no missing person reports from anywhere in this end of the state, so obviously this woman had come from way outside the area to end her life, we all gathered from her short note that she was unable to cope any longer with the inevitable, that her partner had just disappeared like so many other unfortunates that had dared ignore the warnings and had ventured into the Black Mountain.

The desk officer got on the phone and activated a phone tree that had been set up over a dozen years prior. They had found too many bodies over the years, and quite a few people wandering around the mountain in a dazed, unexplainable state.

Due to having experienced this many times before, within twenty minutes, more than twenty-five of the biggest, toughest men living in the area, as well as two volunteer nurses, arrived at the station, and I was told to lead them to where we had found the note. We drove in a caravan to the point where the tree was located, and as soon as we arrived, the men began their search, and the nurses set up their first aid station.

The trees in the area were dried and looked nearly dead. Their leaves, the ones that were still hanging, were brown with tinges of black on their edges. The grass was charred and felled to point away from the mountain. I was surprised that I hadn't noticed those things earlier, but even after I had, none of the "rescuers" seemed to have really noticed them either, or perhaps they were just accustomed to it.

I pointed out the exact tree where the note was found, and the men were all over the area within seconds. They checked the nail holes where the sign had been hung. There was sap flowing from the wound. That meant one thing... the sign had been hung recently, very recently. The cut in the bark was fresh... another sign of a recent event.

"Men, spread out and check further into the bush, this woman or her body has to be around here somewhere," the commander yelled over his megaphone, and with that, the men, me included, started into the bush, not knowing what, if anything, we were going to find. We tried to stay within sight of each other, but soon all of the people were spread so far apart that visual contact was no longer possible.

I was alone for quite a while before I ran into one of the other searchers, Jeff Davidson, who, like me, had nothing to report.

By now, the sun was a little past its apex. We were both getting hungry, so he and I walked over to a log that had been knocked down by some passing storm. I had a turkey sandwich, and he had macaroni salad. It wasn't too hard to figure out that if we shared our food, we had a pretty good meal. He had a GPS in his backpack, so, in addition to eating, we took a reading to see where we were. It showed that we were just about halfway through the bush and getting closer to the mountain. I wasn't sure if a woman set on killing herself would travel as far as we had, but after eating, we decided to keep on walking.

We didn't have to walk very far, about 400 meters away, beneath a nearby tree was a woman's body, it was dehydrated, and above it was a part of a rope, frayed at the end. A quick look showed the other end of the rope was around the neck of the body. This woman had known what she was doing. The noose had thirteen loops and was placed on the left side of the neck. According to documentaries I had seen, this was the most efficient way to die from hanging. It quickly snapped the neck, assuring a quick and somewhat painless death.

I walked around the body and finally found a wallet. The body was that of Amanda Perry from the Sunshine Coast. She was only 34 and, if you can go by the pictures in her wallet, the man was Arthur, her missing husband or boyfriend. Probably a boyfriend, as there was no wedding ring, so we were unsure if they were married or not. We also weren't sure how long she had been dead, but the rope looked fresh, with no weathering, which meant it was new - very new. That meant that she had died recently. I put the wallet in my pocket and took a GPS reading as to the location, and then we started looking around.

The ground was muddy around the site, and there was not one set of footprints as you would expect with a suicide. There were at least three sets of footprints around the body, and two of them led off deeper into the bush and toward the mountain. The thing was, there was something strange about the footprints that neither my partner nor I could put our fingers on, but we started following them anyway.

It was about a half mile that we walked on a muddy trail, following whoever it was that had possibly left the body lying there. The trees faded away about 10 minutes after we resumed walking. The mud turned into chips of pitch-black granite, and shortly after that, they transformed into sharpened rocks of pure blackness. The sky was dark, with gray clouds coming in from the ridges in the next area. The ground was black, and the edges of the rocks were sharp enough to shred the skin off your hands if you were not careful. There was no vegetation at all, not even the mosses you would expect in a warm, dark atmosphere.

On the hard surface, the footprints ended abruptly, but after we discussed it between us, we agreed to continue up the mountain in the same general direction we had been traveling. In the dim light, we could see that the further we traveled, the larger and sharper the rocks became, but at least there was a trail about 3 feet wide weaving between the rocks, and it was going up the mountain at the same rate as we were. By the time we had hit the trail, the only sound that we could hear was the wind blowing around us. The birds had given up making music a long time ago, and we had not even really noticed.

We followed that trail as it got steeper and steeper until we could barely keep our footing, and eventually had actually to crawl, but at least we kept moving up the goddamn mountain. Then we saw something we had not expected... Before us were entrances to several caves, and they appeared to cut deeply into the side of the mountain. We had a brief discussion on the risks of continuing our search to determine the origin of the footprints, and both agreed that we had come this far; we just had to know the answer. So we agreed to continue our investigation, despite all the warnings we had heard that the area was a dangerous, sinister place of no return.

Each of the caves had its own personality. The first was large black granite crystals. Ferns and mosses covered the rocks as well as the floor, making it difficult to stand, let alone walk. The second and third were experiences we had never had before. The stones were rough, nearly rough enough to cut the skin from our bones if we had bumped into them, but the strange thing was... despite the natural coolness of the air in the caves, the rocks were warm. If you moved closer to them, it was as if you went from a cool spring day to the heat of summer in just a few inches. Another thing was that, yes, there were plants inside the cave, but they were all burnt... at least they looked that way. We had no explanation, but they weren't the reason we were there anyway, so we just walked past them.

By the time we reached the cave on the right, it was nearly dark, so we decided not to enter the cave until morning. We settled down outside it for the night. That night, we heard some eerie, strange, and scary animals screaming in the darkness, and others growling and grunting; those sounds somehow seemed a lot closer than the others. That made us extremely nervous, and so we didn't get much sleep that night. To keep up our spirits, we took turns telling jokes and talking about the local horse races and the local whorehouse, which we both as virile bachelors regularly visited, as most of the female population in town were married or wouldn't look at a bloke without a bloody engagement ring or promises of everlasting love. We both agreed, women were great, but marriage and fidelity were not for either of us.

The morning came faster than either of us wanted it to. There was something about the cave that made us wary, even though we had not been inside and did not know what awaited us. We both just had a gut feeling this cave was going to be very different from the others.

We opened our eyes and stepped into a world that was just as dim as the one we had left the day before. The majority of the sounds of the animals we had heard during the night had not faded, which was most unusual to say the least, and the scary growling we had heard during the night had now become almost unbearably loud.

We stepped into the last cave together and found that the air coming from inside was significantly warmer than the air outside or even the air from the other caves. The entrance was totally black. It was not welcoming at all, and we, at least I, had second thoughts, but I knew we had to go in and see what was going on, if anything was happening. Our search for answers over the woman somehow seemed to have dissipated, and now the Black Mountain seemed to have taken actual possession of our souls.

The floor of the cave was smooth and yet dull. There was no light reflecting from the outside. It was darker than dark, and a rank smell emanated from deep within the blackness.

"What's that terrible smell?" my new mate Jeff asked.

"It smells like rotten meat, but not the meat you get at the store. I mean meat from a fresh kill," I replied in a calm voice. Then, to ease both our fears, I brought up the point that dingoes sometimes carry their kills into caves to protect them. Deep in my mind was the memory of a legend passed down for the last 100 years that I couldn't get out of my mind, and I didn't want to discuss. It was just too terrible to think about.

We covered our mouths and noses with cloth; it didn't do much good, but it was at least an effort. The stench was unbearable, but despite it all, we were determined to continue our investigation of the cave, so we continued down a slight grade into the bowels of the mountain, feeling our way down as we went.

There were minerals in the roof and walls of the caves that became increasingly illuminated as we moved further inside.

The further we travelled, the more intense the smell became, as well as the light getting brighter and brighter. Finally, we could see the walls, ceiling, and floor of the cave. There were no more sharp edges. Everything was as smooth as glass and not hot, but comfortably warm. I would guess that the temperature was around 28 degrees, but the high humidity made it feel a lot warmer.

We had already travelled about one mile into the mountain when we saw something that shocked and surprised us... We saw bodies hanging on the wall. They were plump and fresh as a newly dressed chicken, and it was easy to see that their necks had been broken as if they had been hung. I counted three. I couldn't remember how many missing persons that town was looking for, but so far, we had found four bodies and no explanation.

Travelling farther, the smell turned from rotting meat into a kind of bitter smell, and once we turned a corner, we found out why... There was a small group of caves deep within the main cave, and the occupants appeared to be home. I told Jeff to stay where he was as I moved a little closer, and when I did, I saw something that I should have known was there, but never expected to see.

The legend was that the caves on Black Mountain were home to creatures that should have disappeared a long time before humans even thought of walking upright or creating fire. The story was that the caves had an intelligent form of, I guess you could say, a lizard that took humans entrails and blood for food. Well, at that moment, at least the beings were true. The creatures I was watching were tall, almost as tall as I was, and although some walked on two legs, most of them still walked on all fours. Maybe they could go either way. Their skin was scaly and dark green with black stripes running from the backs to their bellies, and their heads were definitely like those of modern-day salamanders, except for a massive set of teeth that kind of reminded me of the alligators down in the New Orleans delta. They had long claws, which came out of the end of each "toe." They looked to be about five to seven inches long, and they did look sharp.

I stood crouched down as I watched at least twelve of the creatures walking around the area. I must have been there for about 30 minutes when the largest of the group started walking back along the trail. Panicked, I hid behind a huge rock, and I hoped that Jeff was doing the same. It took about 5 minutes before the creature returned, dragging one of the bodies I had seen earlier behind him.

The lizard drained the blood from the body to the extent of sucking out the last drop from the heart and veins of its victim. As it did, others came and their long tongues sucked out the entrails, it was such a strange procedure, and it actually seemed like they were doing their best not to cause damage to the actual outer bodies. As all this was happening, the heat in the cave, or something in the air, seemed to "cook" the rest of the body, making it appear extremely dehydrated and almost leather-like. When they were done and everyone was fed, the same lizard that had brought the body in carried it out of the room.

Slowly, I came out of my hiding place and followed the lizard as he moved out of the cave. I beckoned Jeff to follow us as I passed by where he was hiding. The sun was up high in the air as we stepped from the cave. God, it was nice to feel a breeze of sweet air after what we had put up with inside. The lizard travelled down the same trail we had followed up the mountain.

The lizard was slow, very slow, but then dragging the body of a man would slow anything down. It took several hours to reach the wooded area at the base of the mountain. I watched as the lizard passed tree after tree, looking up into each. It looked at a couple of hundred before it stopped, and it placed the body carefully beneath one particular tree.

After the creature left, I walked over to the spot where the body was placed. Looking above the body, I saw a broken rope dangling from a heavy branch.

I looked at Jeff, and he looked at me, and we realized what was happening at the same time. People were committing suicide or getting lost and dying, and the lizards of the mountain were claiming the bodies, devouring what they needed, and returning the rest. We thought about it a minute and I said, "This is nature, and that was all it was. Jeff, I reckon these creatures apparently intended no harm to anyone. They took what neither God nor man wanted. Let's leave them in peace."

Later, we learnt that the bodies found at Black Mountain were usually never claimed or mourned, and were generally buried in unmarked graves. Of course, there was always the exception to the rule like Amanda Perry the woman who had left the note on the tree, but I wonder, if she had known her boyfriend had taken his own life, how that would have affected her, maybe she was better off dead, and possibly united with him now in some happier place, I sure hope so anyway.

After so many years, it was pretty shocking how many suicide deaths must have been concealed by the authorities, yet can you blame them? Possibly, that would have encouraged even more suicides, and who wanted hordes of thrill seekers charging into town, changing the relaxed, easy-going way of life. With all this in mind, Jeff and I agreed to keep quiet about what we had seen and leave the lizards in peace, allowing them to take what they needed to survive. At least the bodies that lay unclaimed meant something to these prehistoric creatures, and I think maybe, in a small way, that justified us not telling anyone what we had seen.

We did agree to report finding the woman's body and the other male body, the prehistoric creature had brought back to its hanging tree, but we never mentioned the lizards, the caves, or anything else that we had found.

Yeah, even today, dehydrated bodies are still occasionally found throughout Black Mountain. Strangely, I never ventured there again, and as far as I know, Jeff and I were the only modern people to see the lizards. We agreed, no matter what their historical importance, they deserved to be left alone and allowed to survive.

So... that's really the end of the story, except to say that Jeff and I have become very close friends. Despite our initial desire during our search to stay single, we have both settled down and married two good Australian women. Regardless of all their many protests and constant curiosity, we never take our wives or kids anywhere near Black Mountain. Let us just hope that one day the lizards run out of bodies to feed on, but then, of course, there might be another problem...

Return of the Mayamah

Just a couple of years ago, a group of young men, numbering about a dozen, graduated from high school. They wanted to celebrate this major step in their lives, but not the way boys usually do. They did not want to get drunk or laid or anything like that. They tried to make some money to get their lives started, and they were willing to work for it. So, they all decided to go mining in Western Australia. Nothing much, just panning for gold in some of the small streams, if they could find any.

They finished their schooling on December 10th. And on December 11th, they were all packed into three cars, and by noon, their hometown, Melbourne, was far behind them and just a fading memory.

After driving all day and night, as the sun rose, they arrived in the city of Port Lincoln, South Australia. It was a nice place, and they decided to stay there for a couple of days to relax and enjoy themselves before they commenced their adventure of panning for gold.

They partied most of the day, and by the time night came, they were all extremely drunk and went back to their hotel room and passed out.

In the morning, one of them, a man named Kelly Joseph, was the first to wake up. He stepped out of his room and headed out to the motel's parking lot to get his cigarettes. He found an old dog sleeping on the hood of his car. It looked like a dingo, but there was something different about it; it was obvious it was not a true blue dingo.

"Come here, boy," Kelly called out to the dog. "Come on, mate; get the hell off my car." He wasn't angry or anything like that; in fact, he thought it was actually funny, especially when the dog looked at him, wagged his tail, and seemed to smile. "Okay, boy, you just stay there and rest, while I go over to the café and get some free tucker." The dog looked at him once again, his tail still wagging madly, then lowered his head and went back to sleep.

Kelly went over to the Motel café and got his complimentary continental breakfast. By the time he was done, the rest of the guys were awake. They joined him for breakfast and then headed to their cars.

They were all joking together when one bloke saw the dog on the car hood." Get off that car, you damn dirty bastard," the young man yelled, as he picked up a stick and threw it at the dog's head. "Didn't you hear me? I said get off the bloody car." The stick flew past the dog, landing harmlessly in the parking lot. "Dirty mongrel, get off the bloody car," he screamed as he lunged for the dog, who was now growling with his teeth fully bared.

The dog was getting ready to attack. Its fur was bristling, its eyes were fixed, and it was crouched down as if it were hunting.

"Mayamah," Kelly yelled at the dog as he ran up to his friend. He had no idea why he yelled that or what it meant, but, as soon as he said it the dog settled back down and it became the dog Kelly had seen earlier." Mayamah... down," he said in a gentle voice. The dog jumped off the car, walked over to Kelly, and sat by his feet.

The rest of the young men in the group then became interested in watching to see what the dog would do next, but there was no growling and no bared teeth. It was as if the dog were a pet.

"What is it with that dog?" one of the men in the group asked.

"I have no idea," Kelly replied. As he started to walk away, he noticed that the dog was never more than two feet away from him. Every move he made... the dog made.

"I guess that dog has adopted you," one of the guys said with a laugh—all of the other guys, except one. Started laughing and agreed that Kell had himself a dog, and they all agreed that there was enough room to take the dog along with them, but providing that Kelly would be the one to take care of him, so when they loaded the cars and Mayamah went contentedly with his new master.

Just before they left, a very old, scruffy man walked over to Kelly's car. He looked at the dog and looked at Kelly.

"You know, mate...," the man stated. "... I've been watching that dog all morning, I reckon. Sometimes you pick the dog, and sometimes the dog picks you. I saw how he reacted to you. I also heard you calling him Mayamah. Why did you call him that?" He enquired.

"To tell the truth," replied Kelly, "I don't have a dinkum clue; it just came like a flash."

The old man smiled and then stretched his arms through the open window, gently stroking the dog on the head. The dog just looked at him, once again wagging his tail, as if he was very pleased to meet the old man.

"Yer know mate, Mayamah is a very special name! Strewth, why this could even be the real Mayamah... if it is, he has a history that goes back a very long time."

"You have seen Mayamah before," Kelly asked.

"No, but I know the stories I heard," the old man said. "It was first written so many years ago, and then told to me by my grandfather, who heard it from his grandfather. It was a mythical dog called Mayamah. My memory is foggy. I am way too old to remember the whole story. What I do remember is that Mayamah is a very unique dog, and if this dog is who I reckon he is, crikey, you've got a very special dog there, so make bloody sure you look after him, mate." Without another word, the old man just turned and walked away, but as he did, he kept looking back and smiling.

"What in the hell was that all about?" Kelly asked. Not one of the group hazarded a guess, and all the dog did was sit there, watching and letting out the very minutest whine. However, other than that, it was strangely silent, except for the sound of car doors closing, engines starting, and the cars moving through the dirt to get back on the main road.

After a few days of traveling by car and ferry, they ended their trip with a twenty-kilometer trek to Lucifer's Gorge. Even after many years, few people knew about the place, and even fewer had ever visited it. The boys had heard about it in a lecture at school on the Earth's hidden places. So naturally in their minds, it was an ideal place to head, no one really knew about Lucifer's Gorge, so they were all convinced it was a safe bet that such an isolated spot, could be a great place to pan for gold or maybe even Opals ... if all they were thinking was true it was an simple way to make some real easy money. They did not doubt the possibility of what they were doing, as years earlier, they had heard of the legend of a group of partying drunks who ventured into the outback and stumbled upon a rock made of solid gold.

The sun was high in the sky when they arrived at Lucifer's Gorge and commenced to set up camp. After they opened a few tins of spam, had a quick feed, and immediately started panning in a stream on the floor of the gorge. Within an hour, they started finding gold dust in their pans, and shortly after that, nuggets about the size of a five-cent piece, and then even a few that were bigger than that.

Unfortunately, their camp was about 800 meters from the place where they were panning, so they just made two or three trips a day back to the camp with their gold findings.

They all were so excited, as every day their finds increased, so, though exhausted, they partied every night. They could not believe their luck. In this day and age, they had actually found gold, and within just a few days, they already had enough gold to buy each of them a pretty nice house and car. They deposited all the gold in an old canvas bag; by then, the gold weighed more than ten pounds, and they made sure to find a great spot to bury it well outside their camp.

One day, they went down to the creek just the same as they always did, but this time, one of them brought a bottle of 151 percent rum with him, and Mayamah went with them that morning. He usually didn't go with them, as his job was to guard the camp, but this day he wagged his tail so hard Kelly soon picked up the idea that his dog wanted a change of pace and to get away with his master for a little bit.

About five hours after they got there, Mayamah's ears perked up. He was hearing something he didn't like. Suddenly, he got up and ran back to camp. His ears were up, and his teeth reflected the day's sun. He got to camp just in time to see three men ransacking the camp. He lunged at one of them, but before he could bite, the intruder grabbed a gun and pointed it at Mayamah's head.

"Back down right now, boy, or it will be the last step you'll ever take," the man with the gun said. Mayamah backed off, he had seen far, far too many times what these nasty sticks had done to humans and also to kangaroos, wild pigs, and snakes. Then the man became angry, screaming at the other two men. "I've seen 'em panning, I've seen loads of gold, where is that gold? " Better find it, if we don't, I will kill this bloody mutt, that will bring 'em running. Flaming hell, where the bloody hell is their gold?" he demanded of the poor dog.

Mayamah stood there, his teeth bared; it was as if he understood every word the man was saying. He stood his ground firmly, waiting for his chance to overpower the man.

The intruder picked up a large tree branch and bashed Mayamah with it. Mayamah was knocked down, but he got up and was about to jump on the man; however, once again, the fire stick was pointed right at him. Suddenly, one of Kelly's young friends, Fred Turner, returned to the camp. He had a bad hangover and wanted to just rest in camp for the afternoon. Immediately, the rifle was pointed at his head.

"Mister, you tell me where you've hidden the gold or I will blow your bloody head off, along with your bloody dog!"

Look, I want to know where the gold is," the gold robber screamed at Fred and even Mayamah. Fred, terrified for his life, immediately passed out on the spot.

Mayamah again bared his teeth, and this time he let out a howl that was so strange and bloodcurdling that every living thing within 500 meters hid and didn't come back out 'til the following morning.

Kelly and the others heard Mayamah's howl down where they were panning. They had only had a couple of drinks, so they were able to run back to the camp. When they got there, they could not believe their eyes. There were three men in their camp... just standing there as if they were frozen. Kelly made a closer look... all three men had been turned to stone... sandstone to be precise. Their clothes, their rifles, knives, and even their sweat, had all been turned to stone.

Fred was still out cold, and they had to throw a bucket of water on him to get him up. He, of course, remembered nothing, except the fact that these men were set on taking the gold, and were sheer killers and would have murdered them all to get it. As Fred was telling them all this, Mayamah walked around the stone figures. Then, he let out a triumphant howl, and once again, Kelly swore that he was smiling.

After that, Mayamah looked at Kelly, then gave a loud bark and ran off into the bush. When he returned 10 minutes later, he was carrying the bag of gold in his mouth his paws were dirty, and it was obvious he had been digging for the canvas bag containing the gold nuggets the young men had panned so hard for. He immediately came over, whimpered softly, and set it at Kelly's feet. Kelly thanked him, patted his head, and then told the others that maybe it was time to leave... maybe there were others who had also seen them pan down by the stream. They all packed up their things and left early the next morning. The gold nuggets were divided evenly into each of their knapsacks.

On the way back to Melbourne, they stopped at the Motel where they had met the old man on their way to Lucifer's Gorge. Mayamah immediately went over to the old man, who gave the dog a pat and said it was nice to have him back. Then Kelly told him all that had happened back at their campsite, and the old man said that he was not at all surprised, as apparently the old myth was true.

"What do you mean by that?" Kelly asked.

The old man explained that in the early 1800s, a small town was attacked by a rival village. "Luckily," the old man stated, "the invaders found the village empty, except for an old dog. They demanded that the dog, which had been left in the village, tell them where the villagers had gone. The dog was able to speak, but refused to reveal its secrets. Anyway, the dog turned every one of those invaders to stone... and everything they owned was also turned to stone." The old man paused in his story, thinking for a minute about how to tell Kelly the name of that dog, then decided to state it simply. "That dog's name was Mayamah."

At that moment, Kelly looked around, and Mayamah was nowhere to be seen; he had just disappeared. For 24 hours, the group searched for Mayamah, but he had utterly vanished, so eventually they had to give up and head back to Melbourne without him.

Occasionally, a story about a dog resembling a dingo roaming the area is spread around.

That day was the last time Mayamah was ever seen again, although in various outback towns over the years, many stone statues suddenly appeared out of nowhere. These statues always leave the local population wondering who puts them there. It is also striking how these stone figures always look like some of the most notorious outlaws and villains in Australian history. Rumors still persist that just before these statues appear, out of nowhere, a dog is seen coming and going with the wind and disappearing like a ghost into the shadows.

New Norfolk's Killer Fish

Thomas Dewitt loved to do nothing but fish. Yeah, he had a job and a good life, and every chance his wife allowed him, which was usually once a month, he went fishing. Living in Harihari, he did a lot of fishing in the Tasman Sea, which wasn't too bad.

On the one day he was allowed to go fishing, he usually caught enough fish to feed his wife and her family for at least a couple of weeks. Eventually, though, he got tired of catching Mako, sharks, bream, and yellowtail. Yeah, they were exciting and fun to see, but Thomas wanted something new.

On the day after his 35th birthday, Thomas got the surprise of his life. His wife came up and offered him a hall pass for a week. She told him that for that week, he would not be married, and he could do whatever he wanted. She thought for sure that he was going to go out with his friends, getting drunk or maybe even hook up with a woman or two, but to her shock, he said that he wanted to go inland and go fishing. That was something she should have expected, but didn't, so she gave her husband her blessing and then went out for the night with her girlfriends.

The first thing he did was to call his two best friends Scott and Alfred. He told them about his hall pass and then he asked if they wanted to go on a fishing trip to New Norfolk with him. Now, Scott's wife, Agatha, wasn't nearly as liberal as Thomas's wife, so he had to beg her to let him go with Thomas. After a couple of hours and a great deal of pleading and hot sex, he was allowed to go with one stipulation... no women. He readily agreed as he really enjoyed going fishing with his two mates, and hell his wife was all he desired anyway. Alfred's wife, on the other hand, was away visiting her sick mother, so he did not have to ask permission. Then, Alfred was told he was not allowed time off from work, but Alfred was not the type who took no for an answer, so he snuck away and went to fishing with his pals, if his boss did not like it, he could stuff his bloody job.

The three of them left Harihari the next morning. Their plan was to fish at New Norfolk just a short distance from Hobart. Once there, they would head to the Derwent River down from where it merged with Lachlan River. Thomas had always heard about how the place was so full of record sized fish that their creels would be loaded down so much that they would have trouble carrying them.

Although it hadn't rained for a couple of weeks it was still the rainy season, so they built their camp about twenty meters from the river's edge. After a few hours with the sound of the river and the crackling of the fire, they were at long last relaxing. The beer and Jack that they had brought with them only added to their much needed freedom and camaraderie.

They woke with the sun, and also with three massive hangovers that lasted until well after breakfast and almost until lunch time. They spent the early afternoon sitting down on the river shore. They weren't the kind of fishermen who just walked down and threw a line into the water. They studied the river, the way it moved, the sounds it made, and even the birds that flew around its banks. They always said if you do all of that, you would know right where the fish were and how to catch them, but, even with all of their observations, they did not see the blue/gray tail of a large creature break the water and then quickly disappear.

The next morning Alfred was the first to wake up. He didn't wake the others; he just got dressed, grabbed his fishing pole, and went down to the river. He caught a couple catfish and some small fish which he threw back. He was there for about an hour when he hooked something and it was so big that it nearly pulled him into the river. "I've got something big," he yelled out to his sleeping friends. "Really big!" His yelling with excitement eventually woke Thomas and Scott, who dressed quickly and ran down to the river bank to help their friend catch a big one.

In less than five minutes, they were at the spot Alfred had been yelling from. They looked around for Alfred, but he was nowhere to be found. They searched everywhere calling for him, but there was no answer. They did find his tackle box and the folding chair he liked to use, but no Alfred, he had suddenly vanished into thin air.

"Where in the hell did that son of a bitch go?" Scott asked.

"I can't imagine,' said Thomas. "I'm worried, why would Alfred, just leave his stuff sitting out like that?"

"Maybe he's playing some kind of joke," Scott said. "He's probably back at camp laughing his ass off at the fools who went looking for him." They went back to camp and their friend wasn't sitting there laughing. He wasn't there at all!"

"He must have walked into town," Thomas said. "I bet he went to get us all brekky before we woke up. He did that when he was a kid, always causing some kind of major disturbance and then just disappear. It always scared his mom to death. A couple times she called the police when she couldn't find him."

"What happened then?" asked Scott

"The police always found him at Maccas and always brought him straight home. He was usually carrying a bag with Egg McMuffins, hash browns and a coffee for his mom whenever they brought him to the door," Thomas said with a laugh. "The cops always lectured him and told him not to do it again, but his mom never punished him so he just did it again and again." They both broke into hysterical laughter over their friend's antics and then made breakfast and they went down and got busy fishing.

They weren't there long when they heard the most hideous noise coming from up the river. It was kind of like a grunt combined with a howl. Neither of them knew what it could have been or even how far away it was but it terrified the both of them. Even so, they didn't quit fishing, but that day their luck sucked. They didn't catch a single thing, so they went back to camp after a few hours, got drunk on a case and half of beer, and passed out even before they had the chance to start a fire.

When they woke up they realized that an entire night had passed. Alfred was still not back. "Oh, he probably met some bird in town and got lucky," Scott said. Thomas laughed and agreed... after all Alfred wasn't very moral and sure as hell wasn't a virgin, so he probably did meet a Sheila and just didn't come back. They were starving so they made some breakfast and got on with their day.

They caught a couple of pretty large fish which they were going to eat that night and, other than that, they were pretty bored and missed Alfred's humor, his sense of fun always set the mood. The only thing they could do to pass the time was to talk, tell jokes and drink. Then they went back to camp, ate the fish, drank some more and, despite the fact that their concern was growing, they went to bed.

The next morning they went fishing again. They had the same luck as they had the previous day, but then things changed. They stopped getting any bites at all. It was like that for about an hour, then all of a sudden Scott got a bite and it was big.

Now, they had heard that there they were giant fish in the area, but they didn't expect to see what Scott had hooked in these waters. His pole was bent nearly in half and his line was moving so fast it was like watching a palm tree in a level five hurricane. More than once he was pulled off of his feet, but he always managed to get back up and keep fighting with whatever he had on his hook. The water foamed up as that fish fought and churned just beneath the surface. Thomas tossed his pole on the ground and went over to help Scott as much as he could.

The fight lasted more than two hours. Scott was exhausted and so was Thomas, neither had ever seen a fish fight as hard as this one. Finally, the fish must have tired and Scott was able to reel it in. Once he got it to the shore what they saw was not a fish... it was a monster. It was more than three meters long, blue grey in color and had a complete set of teeth that any crocodile would love to have. Its mouth was opening and closing as it tried to take in air. The hook was deep in its mouth and there was blood pouring all over the dirt.

"What in the hell is that," Scott yelled. "I have never seen anything like that." Scott said. Thomas didn't... couldn't answer.   He before Scott recognized something shocking. There was a piece of cloth caught in the monster's teeth... It was a piece of the shirt that Alfred had been wearing. It was stained with blood and ripped to shreds, but he was sure that it was Alfred's shirt.

Thomas took a filet knife out of his belt, walked over and stabbed the creature through the back of its head. Its body convulsed and twisted into shapes which he and Scott could never describe, but finally its body went limp and it was dead. When they pried open its ugly mouth, caught in its teeth along with the shirt were shards of human flesh. Both men were sick on the spot; they could not fully comprehend the horrific death Alfred had gone through. Why had they not heard his screams for help, could they have prevented his death - that they could not answer.

Sick to the stomach, they left the creature lying on the shore, knowing they had to go to town and report on Alfred's death. Of course at first the cops didn't believe them, and they were told to stay in town and questioned for two days until the cops went with them to see this "monster" they were talking about. They took them back to where they were fishing. The campsite was still there and just down on the shore was the broken skeleton of the creature. The animals had had a feast on the body, leaving only bones, but the police finally believed their story.

The cloth was still there in its massive jaw and DNA tests on its teeth proved that it was indeed Alfred's flesh.

The police did not need to question Thomas and Scott any further; they were free to go home to Harihari. Later, once all paperwork was completed, they were sent the cloth from the fish's mouth and soon after that a delayed funeral for Alfred was held.

That piece of cloth was placed in the most beautiful black coffin possible, and a memorial service held for Alfred. The coffin containing the cloth was buried at sunset and everyone spoke at the graveside.

The ceremony was memorable, but also very sad indeed as during the ceremony Alfred's wife collapsed and suffered and stroke and never recovered and Alfred's four young daughters were eventually adopted by Thomas and his wife, who had been trying for years to have children.

Thomas heard that the spot where the Derwent River merges with the Lachlan River has been declared a national game preserve. It was a way to stop people from fishing and camping there and meeting the same horrifying fate as Alfred.

Thomas and Scott remain good friends and often go mountain climbing together, but neither man has any desire to ever go fishing again, they are still haunted by the sight of that monster and the memory of Alfred's shirt saturated in blood and the flesh of Alfred's body dangling from its mouth.

Luckily though since then no one else has died at the "hands" of any monster fish and that is at least a good thing.

Mount Gambier's Winged Vampire

Mount Gambier in South Australia is situated 450 kilometers from Adelaide, yet only 17 kilometers from the Victorian border on what they call The Limestone Coast.

The town has grown on the slopes of an inactive volcano, with a population of around 25,000 people. A popular holiday resort that attracts visitors to "The Blue Lake," which changes its colours dramatically each year. A small, friendly, laid back town that has as yet certainly not caught up with the hustle and bustle of Australia's major cities. A beautiful and peaceful stopover, for adventurous tourists, via The Great Ocean Road and the Grampians, to the ever popular Kangaroo Island.

For those living outside of town, it was not quite as peaceful as one would think, one could quite often hear dingoes howling and the night birds screeching, as well as a sudden storm further up in the distant mountains.

For Jonathon Peacock, a farmer living outside of town with his wife Sissy, it was a peaceful and tranquil life. He spent his evenings on his porch drinking Jack Daniels and, unlike his wife and most of the locals, Jonathon never went to bed early, quite often he would walk out into his yard late at night, followed by his cat Tiger, and just listen to the sounds of the bush, stopping now and again to look up at the stars and marvel at the beauty of the Universe. His favorite constellation was Orion, he looked for that every night and he even made a wish on the middle star of Orion's belt. The wishes never came true, but he just kept trying anyway.

On the night of April 7th there was a new moon so, outside of the street lights from the distant town, there was no light at all. It was also extremely quiet, too quiet to be anything but strange. The only light outside the Peacock farm was the porch light and it wasn't that bright. It barely lit the porch much less anything else.

Sometime around midnight, Jonathan finally decided to go to bed. He turned out the porch light, went upstairs, took a nice long bath, got undressed, and slid into bed as his wife woke up for a second and snuggled into his arms. About an hour later, right after he started having a really good dream, he heard his cat howling like he had never heard him howl before then all went deathly silent then a hideous scream came from the area of his chicken coop. It was so loud that he was thrown out of his bed. "What in the hell is that?" he yelled.

His wife had been sound asleep and heard nothing, so she sleepily told him she was sure it was nothing and to come back to bed, no doubt it was probably Tiger fighting with some stray cat. But he knew what he had heard, so instead of listening to her as he usually did, he got his slippers on quickly and ran outside just in time to see something weird and very large running across his yard, it jumped over the fence and then it was gone.

He couldn't even make a guess as to what it was but, when he got to his chicken coop, he saw it had been torn apart and although most of the chickens were okay, quite a few were dead and covered with blood.

Then, Jon got a terrible shock to discover his cat Tiger's head was lying on the ground, but he could find nothing else the rest of his body was gone. Jonathan reeled in shock. Tiger was old, but he and Sissy had had Tiger since a kitten, Jon felt so sickened he threw up. He did not know how he was going to tell his wife, she doted on old Tiger. He didn't touch anything, except to lay a towel over what remained of Tiger, and then he went inside the house, told his wife about the chickens being slaughtered, and then went to call the police. Usually he would not have done this, but because of the way Tiger had been murdered, and the destruction of the chicken coop, Jonathan wanted whatever or whoever had done this, shot and killed.

The cops showed up early in the morning. Unfortunately they didn't really consider a decapitated cat, a destroyed chicken coop, or the mutilation of a few chickens a serious crime, so they had taken their time getting there. Once they did finally arrive, they investigated the best that they could. They searched the area and took photos of the chicken coop which of course was proof of some kind of vicious animal attacking the chickens, which seemed somehow drained of blood; they found the rooster's comb beside the fence, but no other sign of the missing rooster. They also found some strange footprints on the ground, but of course they could have been made by any kind of animal... the prints were quite distorted, so the police dismissed them and left, taking three of the chickens with them.

Still reeling from the slaughter of Tiger, after the police left, Jonathan buried his cat's head behind the old white gum, and then went inside to tell his wife about the police visit. He found her once again searching the house for Tiger; he didn't have the heart to tell her the truth, not at the moment anyway. Tiger had gone wandering before, so he assured her as the chicken coop was being attacked, he had probably run off in fright.

The night before, just after he returned to the house, Jonathan had told Sissy all he had seen without mentioning the fact Tiger had been decapitated, but as he now spoke Sissy was not fooled, Tiger was missing, and she could see how upset her husband had been when he had come into the house. In her heart, she knew she would never see her beloved cat again, but she accepted that fact and said nothing more to Jonathan. Something awful had happened to Tiger and she knew it, but did not really want to know what!

Jonathan bought a new rooster and started building a new chicken coop. After that, he spent every night out on his porch with a rifle borrowed from a friend. He had decided to sleep for part of the day after doing all his chores, and stay up all night on the porch, waiting for the creature's return. Whatever that thing was, Tiger had not deserved the pain he must have suffered, and whatever the hell it was, that bloody creature sure wasn't going to get any more of his chickens. He also was going to make damn sure it wasn't ever going to escape back over that fence, if it did manage to get onto his property.

Sissy kept him company 'till about 10 pm every evening and then she went off to bed. So for twenty nine days he never saw or heard anything. The nights were so peaceful that a lot of the time he was having a lot of trouble staying awake, but outside of a couple of ten minute naps, he managed to stay awake the entire time.

The night of the thirtieth day it was as dark as pitch, as the moon was once again in its new phase. Jonathan was in his usual place in his Dad's old rocking chair with his bottle of Jack and the rifle by his side by his side. He hadn't touched any Jack since his wife, Sissy, had gone to bed, so, except for dozing off now and again, he was fairly aware of what was happening.

Shortly after one in the morning, he heard a noise coming from the side of his house. It sounded like the chicken coop again, so he grabbed his rifle and took off running. As soon as he turned the corner, he found himself looking at whatever it was. When it saw him it turned and started running off toward the fence. It was fast... a lot faster than it was the last time he'd seen it, but even so Jon had the time to raise the borrowed rifle to his shoulder and fire. His aim was slightly off, but at least the bullet hit this huge creature in the shoulder, but even that didn't slow it down... not in the least! The last thing Jonathan saw of the creature that night was it leaping over the fence, its huge wings opening, and the monster bat- like creature flying off into the night.

Once again the police were called, and just like the last time they took some of the newly killed chickens, due to their blood drained bodies, and were again ready to leave, when Jon showed them something new. In the spot where he hit the creature they found a small piece of black flesh and a spot of blood in the grass. They cut a blade of grass with the blood on it and the piece of flesh and took those with them as well. "We'll be getting in touch," one of the officers said.

"Yeah, right," Jonathan said without even trying to hide his skepticism. Then he just stood and watched as they drove away.

Once again, he took his post every night smoking and drinking, to hell with his darling Sissy getting so concerned over his health and, his now uncontrollable obsession to kill this monstrous birdlike creature. Yet despite all his waiting, night after night, the creature was nowhere to be seen.

As each night continued to pass in peace and quiet, it suddenly occurred to Jonathan, that he had got it all wrong. The first time he had seen the creature, it was a new moon. The second time it had come back... once again, it was a new moon.

So, he suddenly realized, that creature must only come out when the moon was new. Maybe the light from the moon bothered it or something, but that wouldn't happen when the moon was new. There was no light shining from it. It needed the darkness to come out. After that, Jonathan started going back to bed somewhat earlier much to his wife's delight.

On the thirtieth day, he called a bunch of his friends, borrowed some guns from the police department, and he stationed everyone in strategic positions around his farm. The moon was a new moon, but that night it had a slight red glow to it. No one knew why, but it was there.

Sometime around 1:30 there was that noise Jonathan had heard before. Once again, it was by the chicken coop. All of the men saw the creature bent over the chickens. It was feeding again. Suddenly one of the men fired, hitting the creature in the back, right between its shoulder blades. It raised its head to the sky and it screamed as loud as it could. Its wings opened. Peacock saw the full extent of the creature for the first time. It must have been six feet tall and its wings spread out to a length of nearly twenty feet.

"Oh, my God!" Jon exclaimed as all of the men opened fire. Bullet after bullet entered the creature. It shook with each hit, but it did not go down. Its eyes were glowing a bright, demonic green, and there was blood pouring from its mouth. The men kept firing again and again, reloading faster than they ever had before.

Finally, the creature started running toward the fence. It managed to get to the fence before it fell over, smashing its head into the ground. The wings fell limp and the glow from its eyes disappeared. The creature was dead.

Both the town police as well as the South Australia State Police arrived at the scene in less than twenty minutes. They took back all the borrowed rifles and then went with Jonathan and his friends to look at the creature. It was large to say the least. Their official report said that the creature had a seventeen foot wingspan, extra-large canine teeth, and a set of the most vicious looking claws at the tip of each wing. Then the report went on to say that, under official wording, the creature was considered to be a true and actual vampire.

The body was taken away that night and destroyed, but for anyone interested in vampires and pre-historic creatures, you can still see its skull in a museum near Mount Gambier

Jonathan Peacock never lost another chicken, and a few weeks after the monster vampire bats destruction, a stray kitten landed on Jonathan and Sissy's porch and the newly named Tiny Tiger soon found himself a new home, filled with love and all creature comforts.

Of course, there is always a chance that someday another vampire will appear out of the sky and rip the Tiny Tiger's head off... but for now the skies are clear and everything is back to normal in Mount Gambier.

The Ghosts of Geelong Gaol

Here is something that they never tell you. You should know it, but my wife, Helena, and I certainly did not, and we never dreamed how bizarre and scary it would be when we took the last tour of the Geelong Gaol.

The guide was very informative, and it was all very interesting, but a little too long. We made the mistake of deciding to leave the scheduled tour, and told the guide that Helena was not feeling well and needed to go. He pointed the way out, and we pretended to head in that direction, but the moment we were out of his sight, we decided to explore things we had not seen, and so we wandered off by ourselves. We had heard so many eerie stories about the things that went on there, so we impulsively decided to check it out without the tour guide telling us things we had already read about on Google.

We knew the gaol was big, but stupidly, we did not realize how enormous it was… and suddenly we were lost and could not find our way out. Unfortunately, our tour was the last one of the day, and as we had said we were leaving, no doubt the guide really thought we had gone and did not come looking for us when the jail was closed and all the doors locked. Therefore, due to our own stupidity, we were trapped inside.

Instantly, the doors closed, and all the lights were turned off, leaving only the dim security lights to illuminate the area. It was a sudden and scary feeling as we wandered through the hallways, trying to find our way out. The place had a strong history of murders, suicides, and it was reported that even some ghost guards still roamed the halls more than 150 years after the gaol had first begun taking in prisoners.

It felt extremely creepy; as we walked around, it was deadly quiet. Still, the deathly silence was suddenly shattered by strange echoes that, at first, Helena thought were coming from the streets around the prison. However, I swore that I could hear something that sounded like chains dragging, but I didn't dare tell Helena this; she was scared enough already.

In fact, Helena was not happy at all; she had a tight hold of my hand and was actually shivering, but then, luckily, things soon went back to normal for her after she found a vending machine by the entrance door and an open cashier's office. After buying several items from the vending machine, she decided to sit in the office waiting for me with her Coke, chips, and Cherry Ripe while I walked around exploring the rest of the prison. The normality of the vending machine and the office had calmed her right down, so I was not at all worried about leaving her there. If she needed me, she could call out. Now that the place was empty of tourists, every sound seemed to echo everywhere.

As I walked around, I could still hear the creepy sounds that I had heard earlier, so I started thinking that maybe it was the building settling or something like that, but then suddenly it seemed to be coming from everywhere and not just one place. Perhaps a guard had returned or something else had happened.

"Hello," I called out, but all I got in reply was my wife answering with her own hello. It sure eased the tension I was feeling at that moment, so I laughed and called her a smart-ass.

I don't know if she heard that or not, but I figured that I would find that out when I got back. Anyway, I just kept walking deeper into one of the cell blocks.

I looked into each of the cells as I passed, and they all sent shudders through my body. How could anyone have survived living in this hell? Today, they don't even keep animals in the zoo to live in such conditions. People protest vehemently against cruelty to animals, but I guess prisoners in those early years in Australia were regarded as a worse lot than any animal! I must admit that in my later years, I find it hard to comprehend man's inhumanity to one's fellow human beings.

Suddenly, as I continued further along the passageway, there was one cell for some reason that particularly caught my attention. I was drawn to it as if by a magnet. It was completely empty, except for the skeleton of a bunk and a toilet. However, what I noticed most were the walls. Someone had carved hundreds of scratches into the stone walls. There were hundreds, maybe even thousands… I wasn't able to count them all. Whoever it was took time to scratch marks deep enough so that I could see them in the faint light coming in through a very small window. Then it came to me. Whoever this was… they must have spent years locked in this small cell with no hope and no life to speak of.

"It was a long time," a voice said from behind me. I jumped back in fright and looked around, expecting to see a security guard, but there was no one there. I immediately left the cell and made a quick check in the hallway; there was no one there either.

Gather all my courage, but sweating profusely, I walked back into the cell and whispered, "Who is that," I asked. Then I felt a surge of relief, as I suddenly thought that maybe Helena was playing around again, but then the fear returned as I realized it was a man's voice that had spoken to me. That was one thing I was sure of… it was a man's voice.

Immediately, I became concerned for my wife, so I yelled, "Helena, are you still where you were?"

"Yeah, why?" came back my wife's reply. "What's wrong? Are you hearing things again?" I could hear a slight laugh in her voice. God, she could be a real pain in the ass. If I haven't been so in love with her... I had hoped that some ghost would have appeared and given her a real fright.

"It is not her, it is me, she'll be fine, I assure you, we will not go near her!" the voice said as if it could hear everything that I was thinking. It also made me shudder; this was really terrifying stuff. These were not your ordinary ghosts, haunting houses through some personal tragedy; some of the people incarcerated here were mass murderers. Once again, my thoughts were read as the voice said.

"Do not worry; I was not in here for a violent crime. I was innocent, but I never made it out again." By now, I was sweating even more profusely, my nerves were on edge, and my heart was pounding out of control. I tell you, I was nearly peeing in my pants. I had never experienced anything like it, yet I couldn't run; my feet were frozen where I stood.

"Who are you?" I asked. I wasn't playing, so even though I was scared shitless, part of me was also inquisitive and really wanted to know who this person was and why he was still here as a spirit serving time in a prison that closed so very long ago.

"I'm afraid I do not know who I am," the voice said. "I forgot my name long ago. My life was spent in orphanages and gaols so I was never really a person... just an object to be punished for simply being who I am... or rather who I was."

I have to tell you, as I listened, it was really weird talking to someone who wasn't there. However, even though it was all so bizarre, he really seemed like a decent, nonviolent ghost, so I did my best to calm my nerves and make the most of the situation.

So, I gave him my full attention and listened to all he had to say. His voice was not at all scary, yet it was very frail and sounded both angry and frustrated.

"I was arrested for a murder I didn't commit and sentenced to life in prison here, but that didn't last long... maybe five years, but I tell you those five years were pure hell."

"How bad?" I asked.

"The guards were vindictive fiends, and believe me, so were most of the prisoners here; they all hated me cause I had, from the very first, always protested my bloody innocence, so they all attacked me to make matters even worse. They put me in this cell right next door to James Ross. I can tell you he made my life a living hell."

I could hear the pain in this man's voice as he continued to tell me his story. "The night after he was executed, he came into my cell and he roughed me up real bad. It was so bad that I was taken to the hospital, and I died there the next morning."

As he kept talking, I saw a mist appear before me, it kind of paced back and forth in the cell.

"The nursing staff asked who beat me, but when I told them it was the ghost of James Ross, they thought I was crazy and injected me with laudanum to help me get my mind straight. It didn't work, but it made my death a lot more pleasant. "

I had heard of laudanum, and from what I heard, it wasn't a good thing to be put on, since odds were that you were going to die from using it. Then I asked him what I knew had to be asked… "Why didn't they eventually release you if you were innocent of the crime they said you did?"

"Mate, to tell the truth, I was somewhat of a pain in the ass to the territorial leaders I was fighting for justice for all mistreated and sodomized orphans, so when they had an unsolved murder, to shut me up, they blamed it on me, and the courts went along with them," he cried out. "I never got justice, so I just threw in me bloody towel and tried to settle in here and accept my fate, figured that fighting was bloody useless."

I did understand what he was saying… sometimes it is better just to give up and take what life hands you. Sometimes, it can even hand you apples instead of lemons. But I certainly understood that was not what had happened here.

Reading my mind once again, he stated, "Well, let me assure you I got nothing but lemons! I heard that they even got proof that I was innocent a few days before I died, but the cads never did anything about it... except that they apparently buried the information behind a brick in a wall at the town square."

Then I quickly realized why he had revealed himself to me, as he asked me if I would go and find those papers and finally clear his name.

I told him that I would try my very best, but I couldn't promise anything; I would just try. Immediately, I made this promise, he instantly stopped speaking to me.

I called out several times to him, but there was no reply; all was suddenly silent, no chains rattling, nothing, but deadly screaming silence.

Quickly, I made my way back to Helena. She looked at me and, instead of asking me where I had been, she snapped that I had utterly forgotten her and she needed more money for some more soft drinks. I guess I did leave her for far too long, but I didn't argue. I just apologized and went off to get her a Coke.

As I put the money in the machine, I saw several mists and shadows, but none of them tried to make contact with me, as my thoughts were still with the spirit I had been talking to earlier and how I could help him.

During the rest of the night, we slept together in one of the nearby cells. During the night, I saw a ghost guard pass by a few times; luckily, Helena did not see it, nor did she hear the usual chains rattling, but she did hear screams and voices, so my wife clung desperately to me all night. Eventually, she did sleep a little, but I just lay there in that rotten hell hole thinking about all that had occurred, and the dastardly horrors that must have taken place in this prison over the years.

In the morning, we both felt blessed when the sun came up and some real people showed up to get the gaol ready for the day. "What are the two of you doing in here?" one of the men asked when they found us.

We explained that we had lost the tour group and had been locked in. "Well, you have to leave," he said. We agreed, but before we left, I asked about the man I had spoken to.

"He told me that he was innocent, and there was proof on a wall in town that had the proof of that." I said.

"Oh, old Henry, at it again, eh!" the man said. "Sorry mate, I hate to burst your balloon, but quite a few people have talked about chatting with old Henry."

"He said he was killed by a man named Ross?" I said in the form of a question.

"Ross was long dead when old Henry died," the man replied. "Ross was executed in 1856... old Henry died three years later in 1859. There was no way Ross killed him."

"What about the letter behind the wall?" I asked.

The man laughed and said that the site where the "wall" was now part of a Big W out on Malop Street. "Mate, that wall was torn down years ago, and I assure you there were no papers hidden in, on, or under it or anywhere else around the area," he said. "Old Henry has been trying to prove a conspiracy for the last 157 years. He was found guilty... the evidence proved it... By the way, did Henry tell you he was convicted of being a mass murderer of orphan children? Nope, by the shocked look on your face, I guess not! He usually leaves that part out; apparently, old Henry was quite eccentric and believed he was doing a kindness by saving orphans from a life of hardship, so in his mind, he was utterly innocent. Because of this, the judge took pity on him, so instead of death he was sentenced to life in prison. He eventually died a natural death."

The man then offered me a copy of Henry's prison records to prove everything the spirit had told me was a crock.

He then escorted us back to the front door, where he did the strangest thing... he apologized for any inconvenience the ghost may have caused us. "I hope you come back again sometime," he said. "But next time, please stay with the group and don't wander off. I am sure you'll see your share of ghosts and have fun in the meantime." Then he handed me and Helena a couple of free passes as he closed the doors behind us.

My thoughts often go back to the conversation I had with that spirit. I wonder if maybe he was telling the truth and there is STILL a cover-up going on but, there was no paper and the doctor said he died a natural death so the questions will always be there.

Still, despite my wishing it was so, I am not going to be the one to find out the truth... if the story wasn't just a crazy murderer trying to be free, then one day may his soul rest in peace. For now, I do know one thing... Old Henry is still there serving his time, and he will be for a very long time to come. If he was guilty after all, I just hope that the young orphan spirits he possibly killed, never find out where Henry is, or our old Henry may be in for a lot of outraged orphan retribution!

Marsupial Tigers of Queensland

More than 30,000 years ago, in the area now called Queensland, large Marsupial Tigers roamed the land, coexisting with the first humans who settled on the Australian continent. Obviously, something happened between the humans and tigers, as they eventually faded out of sight and were thought to be extinct, at least that is what everyone believed. Then, in 1871, one was seen and its presence recorded. Legend then had it that a few still survived in isolated pockets of Queensland.

In 1964, the small town of Pondsworth, Queensland, found out for sure that these marsupial tigers were still alive and wandering the forests around their village. It was reported that a big cat was seen rummaging through a garbage can at one of the farms just outside town.

The old woman who owned the farm described it as much bigger than any dog she had ever seen. It was orange with black stripes on its hind quarters, hand-like paws with giant claws, and razor-sharp teeth. She said that when she made a slight noise, the animal roared, flashed its teeth, and ran off into a nearby grove of trees. She immediately called the police on her phone, but unfortunately, they thought she was most likely short-sighted or drunk and had possibly seen one of the larger neighborhood feral cats, which were always seeking food in the local garbage bins.

The old dingbat was always complaining about her ransacked chicken coop; no doubt she had imagined the whole thing. So, naturally, the local constable in charge never bothered to investigate further.

Two nights later, the old woman's house was surrounded by a pack of at least six of these creatures. They circled around the house, and every once in a while, one would let out a blood-curdling howl. The old woman was there by herself and was far too terrified to go outside, so she just looked out the window, watching them. Even just looking at them sent shivers through her old body, and her heart would not stop racing. Her new telephone was suddenly not working, so there was no way she could call for help.

As one hostile creature looked up at her window and howled, she now wished she had shut up and paid her phone bill, instead of protesting their poor service and reception. Perhaps they had even had the nerve to cut off her phone, or maybe it was just the phone itself.

Whatever it was, right now she wished she had not been so foolish, thinking she did not really care if she had this modern contraption or not.

As the tigers continued to circle the house, she became more terrified. Nothing usually rattled her, but now she was as scared as she had ever been in her entire life! As she prayed to the good Lord to save her, she also cursed her own stupidity. She couldn't even phone her son or neighbor to come to her rescue. She was genuinely terrified and utterly alone.

The tigers continued to circle for nearly an hour before one came onto the porch and ripped through the screen door. Luckily, the front door was closed, so the old woman was safe for the moment, but she knew, oh how she knew, that it wouldn't be for long. Minute after minute, the animals clawed at her door until it was so weakened that they were able to break through it. Within seconds, the 84-year-old woman was dead.

Her flesh was ripped from her body, and the tigers devoured everything they could eat. Her blood streaked the walls and floor, and their bite was so powerful that every bone in her body was not just broken... they were shattered and strewn all over the room. This was a scene so horrific that no one in their right mind could ever imagine.

Her body was found by her distraught son several days later. By the time it was found, several farmers had reported seeing Tigers, and the old lady's neighbors on their farm ten kilometers away had also been attacked and killed. Not one of them escaped; the father, mother, and two kids... all dead!

These Queensland tigers had tasted human blood, and it seemed that they had developed a new love for it. The police, federal troops, as well as local citizens, searched the area to try to find and kill the tigers, but as always, they were nowhere to be seen. The police did find a couple of dead hitchhikers who had also been ripped apart; there were even some blood trails where the hitchhikers' blood had dripped from one of the tiger's drooling mouths, but unfortunately, nothing else.

Deep in the bush their growls were heard from time to time, but, when the men reached the area where the growls came from... There was nothing there. They searched for days, but no matter what they did, including setting traps, nothing led them any closer to these elusive, bloodthirsty animals.

There were more attacks, and then finally, there was a survivor. A child of about 11 years, this little girl was very badly mauled, but luckily, she managed to get away. She collapsed on the outskirts of the town and was soon found by a local farmer, and was immediately taken to the local hospital. Her wounds were massive, covering about sixty percent of her body, but she was alive. After a 48-hour surgery and a couple of days of rest, she was able to tell her story.

"We all went to bed. I remember the moon was bright. I could see it in my window," she said. "I was still awake, and I heard something break a window downstairs. My dad yelled for all of us to hide when he went downstairs with a cricket bat. I hid under my bed. Whatever they were, they roared like lions. I heard my father suddenly scream, and then I couldn't hear him anymore. Then I heard a loud clicking coming up the steps. It kept coming and coming." The young girl started to cry, remembering the horror of it all. Before she continued, the town's doctor gave her a tranquilizer to calm her down a little, as she continued her story. "They went into my mum and dad's room. My mum never had a chance. I heard her screaming; it was so horrible. Then, suddenly, there was only silence. They had killed her that fast. Then I heard them sniffing and heading for my room. It was like a pet dog does when you're offering it food. I tried to be as quiet as possible, but one of them found me. I was terrified; they had killed my parents, and now it was my turn. I was terrified, but I tried to remain strong. I yelled at them and hit one of them as hard as I could with a tennis racket I had under my bed, but it bit me anyway. Then, one after another... they bit me, clawed at me, and were tearing at my throat, but I fought them off and gathered enough strength to drag myself to my wardrobe, crawl in, and bar the door. They tried to break the door and get in, but I fought for my life, holding the door tight every time they tried. One managed to claw through it, but something must have distracted them, as finally, they just left. I was so afraid that I didn't come out till the next morning. I went looking for my mum's body, but she was gone. Her bed was full of blood. So was my dad's. I don't know what exactly happened to them." The tears started falling silently as this brave little girl put her head back on the hospital pillow, and after being given another injection by the doctor, soon fell asleep.

    The entire town was in an uproar, which then commenced an even more elaborate search of every farm in the area. The press, as always, was having a field day, attacking the incompetence of the police and military, but still not one beast was sighted.

    The following week as the hysteria mounted, and while hundreds were out in the bush searching, the pack of blood thirsty marsupial tigers suddenly appeared from nowhere and wandered into the town centre. As they walked down the street, the people started screaming hysterically, running for cover, and diving into the nearby stores. Luckily, it was the middle of the day, so all of the town's kids were still in school; the school had been notified to lock the buildings down. That meant that nothing could get in and no one could get out.

Phone calls were made, and the police and military were summoned back to town. The people were rightfully frightened, and they needed immediate help. The last phone call came from the elementary school.

The tigers were surrounding the school, and at least one had managed to get in through the security doors. It wasn't doing anything; it was just walking the halls, looking, sniffing the air, and basically just being a cat. While walking around the school, one of the tigers suddenly gave out a horrendous roar, and when it did, the petrified children started crying hysterically. The tiger's ears perked up as it searched the building for the source of the sound. Finally, it tracked down the source of the noise. The tiger tried to break through the door to the children. But luckily, it was made of metal, so its efforts amounted to nothing. The kids were safe behind the door, so the tiger went back outside, rejoined the group, and they all ran off back into town.

The army had now sealed off the town and positioned guards at every intersection, and they were armed to the teeth, so once they spotted the first tiger, they opened fire with everything they had. In less than a second, the cat fell to the ground, and the others ran off, howling, growling, and in an advanced state of rage. The soldiers chased them, but once again, they were nowhere to be found.

"This is ridiculous," one of the soldiers said in frustration. "We should be able to catch these damn cats!" The rest of them agreed, but not one laughed or even said anything; they just walked over and looked at the fallen animal. It was still breathing, so one of the soldiers took his rifle, placed the barrel on the tiger's head, and pulled the trigger.

The others didn't run too far. It seemed as though they had regrouped and decided to return to the town. They then ran through the city, clawing at everyone they saw. The blood filled the gutters, and the screams of the attacked people filled the air. Finally, the tigers were surrounded at the intersection of Main Street and Johnstown Terrace. There were more than one hundred rifles pointed at the five cats. Then suddenly, the command came to fire.

Every rifle fired its entire clip. The tigers fell one by one, each taking its last breath within just a few seconds.

No one can tell you for sure whether those were the last of the marsupial tigers in Australia or not. There is still talk of them still being seen as far away as Tasmania. If those marsupial tigers shot that day were the last of their kind, then the people of Queensland can sleep in peace. If not... keep an eye on the forest and bushland... There may be something out there watching you, just waiting for its chance to devour you.

The Sound of the Bullroarer

One of the most sacred items of the Outback Aboriginal people is the bullroarer. It is used for ceremonies and it is illegal for a woman, any woman to touch this mystical item. To describe a bullroarer is really simple. It is a long piece of wood with a rope on one end and intricate designs down its entire length. When it is swung, it makes a humming sound that is like nothing else on Earth. Because it is sacred and has powers that can be either positive or negative, it is forbidden for women to touch as that releases the very negative spirits.

Back in October 1995, George Towner, his wife Sara, and their two young children, Kevin, who was ten, and Damian, who had just turned eight, decided to go into the outback for the school holidays. They decided to camp in the Central Desert in Australia's Northern Territory, which was more than 200 kilometers from the nearest town. Luckily it was not utterly isolated, as there were one or two Aboriginal settlements throughout the area.

George Towner was an aboriginal, who was adopted by Alice and Rodney Towner as a baby, and raised in Sydney, but he always had a desire to see and experience the culture he was taken from, and this trip was going to give him that opportunity and much more.

The area was stark to say the least. There were a few trees, a stream and a lot of open space. That was what the family was looking for... a place where they could be alone without the Internet or the constant ringing of a cell phone.

Having lived in Sydney since they were married, George and Sara found this place, deserted as it was a paradise, and for Sara, who had been born and raised in New York City this place was a pure unexpected pleasure.

Once they settled in the area, George tried to become friendly with the local aborigines, but they stayed their distance and it wasn't 'til they knew that George was one of them, part of the lost generation, that the local tribe accepted him and became friendly.

It was not long before they began to teach George the traditional ways, and how to hunt, and brought the family food ranging from roast kangaroo, emu, and even roasted snake. They showed George where water sources were and how to survive on food the desert provided. George knew he had been really accepted when the head of the settlement came over to invite him to a Bora, a ceremony they were having that evening to initiate some of the younger boys into manhood.

Sara begged George to take her with him, George knew it was forbidden for a woman to be there, but he was worried Sara would follow him; at least if she went with him to the camp she would be safe with the women watching her.

The Bora ceremony was to be held close by, so they tucked their children into the sleeping bags, told them a story and waited till they were asleep. As soon as their eyes closed, and Sara and George were sure the boys were asleep, they ordered their two dogs to guard the children, a duty the dogs had been trained to do, ever since the children were born. Then George and Sara walked the half mile to the camp village. They got there right on time.

When they arrived at the camp, Sara was sent to spend time with the women. Despite, all of her objections, she was not given a choice. She had to leave. What was coming was for men's eyes only, and George was going to be one of the few outsiders from the city to be allowed to observe.

George was taken to a secluded spot not far from the settlement camp. The ritual George was to witness began with the men dressed with body decoration, singing and dancing and storytelling, ceremonial traditions that were already ancient when the first white men set foot on the continent. In the distance he could hear the music of the bullroarer. The music mated with the sounds of the desert breeze drifting across the plains. The sound was strangely mystifying. George later said that he was drawn into a world where beauty and peace surrounded him. He just sat there for God knows how long just listening to the music.

After several hours, one by one the boys, fifteen or sixteen years of age, walked into the circle. They were guided in, laid down on the ground and held by two men.

A religious man walked out with a very, very sharp dagger. The boys were held tightly as the man walked over, bowed, and circumcised each one boy after the other. It was a centuries old tradition and the boys knew that it was coming, secretly some were a little afraid, but were also determined to be brave, ready for their pathway to manhood. Even so, one did scream and writhe a little as the knife cut away his foreskin.

"They are not finished yet," one of the elders explained to George.

"What else do you have to do?" George asked.

"They come back in another week for the second part of the initiation." he said. "When they come back in seven days a hole is cut through their penis and a rod is inserted to keep the wound from healing over. George, this is a very sacred ceremony you must never tell anyone about what you have seen or heard here... especially not a woman. This was not meant for them to know." George promised as he rose from his seat. No one would ever hear about what he was honored enough to see.

I'm glad I am not going to be here for that second ceremony, George thought. He could feel his dinner coming back up. What he had seen and heard was too much for him, but he stuck it out.

After the ceremony, George and the tribal leader walked back to the camp. There was a celebration going on to celebrate those boys starting on their way to manhood. Sara rejoined George and asked what happened out in the wilderness. He replied that he promised that he would never tell, but she insisted, but the more she asked the more he refused to answer.

"George, never forget you are part of this community," the most revered elder said as he walked over to them, as George turned around the old man handed him a musical instrument.

"What is it," George asked.

"It is my lost son's bullroarer," the old man replied. "I wish for you to have it as a gift, you could be my lost grandson for all I know, the missionaries stole our children and it is a day of rejoicing when one of you returns to their indigenous roots." George took it happily and held it tightly in his hand. As he did, Sara started reaching for it.

"Stop," the old man yelled as George pulled the instrument away from her. "You are forbidden to touch a bullroarer," the old man stated angrily. "It is for men only... you must understand that." Sara didn't truly understand, but she did back off immediately the look in the old man's eyes frightened her.

On the way back to the campsite George was playing with his new gift, swinging it as he tried to get the same music to come out that he had heard earlier. It was close... really close... but it still didn't sound the same.

The entire time he was whizzing the bullroarer, Sara kept bugging and bugging him for to know what exactly happened at the Bora, and she also kept on insisting she wanted a turn to make music too. "C'mon, darling," she said with a persistent cooing feminine whine. "Just let me know what happened... please, Georgie please, please!!!" George just ignored her. He was far too interested in the notes the bullroarer was making.

They were beautiful to say the least, but unfortunately still not quite right.

"Please, honey bunny, if you won't tell me what happened at the ceremony... well, at least let me try that thing." Once again George shook his head. After that Sara really became insistent. Once again George said no, but this time he became just as adamant as his wife..

They were about fifty yards away from the camp when Mother Nature made her call on George. It came on hard and fast so he didn't have time to wait to get back to camp. Unfortunately, he didn't have the time to think either. He tossed his pack to Sara, along with the bullroarer, as he ran off into some grass to relieve his problem. A second later, Sara heard, "Oh shit!" as George suddenly realized what he had done.

Sara started laughing as she held the bullroarer into the air and, started swinging. The music that came out was atrocious. It was more like the chant of demons rather than music. Actually, the sound was so bad that a flock of lorikeets in a distant tree all took off at the same time. Sara saw that. She guessed that there may have been a thousand or more birds in that tree, but it was now completely empty. More than a few of them crapped all over George on their way out... not the greatest thing to happen, it made George angry and made Sara laugh, so playing with George's little toy was well worth it. (She knew he would be angry, but luckily his anger never lasted long, he was a good husband and Sara loved him dearly!).

She was truly surprised, when George ran out of the grass in a genuine panic, grabbed the bullroarer out of her hands, and held it as far away from her grasp as he could. "Why would you do that," he yelled at her. "Didn't you hear that man? He said women were forbidden to touch this damn thing. Sara, this is very serious you have no idea what it can do! You have set off negative spirits, how could you possibly be so stupid!"

Sara was immediately very sorry she had upset George so, she had only been having fun, but seeing him so upset she felt terrible.

They walked back to their campsite in silence, and when they got there everything was strangely quiet, even the dogs did not bounce out of the bushes with their usual welcome. Suddenly feeling utterly drained and exhausted, Sara sat down by their extinguished camp fire, while her husband starting collecting some wood to re-light it again. Then Sara's motherly instincts kicked in, and she immediately got up and went over to check on the kids.

 The dogs were nowhere to be seen, yet the tent flap was still zipped and as usual it was hard to open... she jiggled the zipper a couple of times and it slid down. Looking in she got a terrible shock. "Darling," she screamed. "George, the kids are gone! They're not here! Where are our kids? Do you think they could have gone to the toilet? Oh God, we should never have left them. Oh George, where are our boys!"

"What?" George yelled as he dropped the wood he was carrying and came running over to the tent.

"The boys they aren't here," she screamed in panic. "What happened to them... my God, where are our boys!"

George tore the tent apart, searching for some clue to where the boys could have gone. In fact, there was really no signs that they had been there at all, everything was gone except for the two empty sleeping bags. No, there were absolutely no signs of Kevin or Damien, or the dogs, or where they all could have gone. It was as if they all had not existed, which made George and Sara feel even more frantic.

They both spent the rest of the night searching the entire an area around the campsite, they even went way, way into the bush looking for possible tracks, but there was no sign of their two boys. No sign at all, the strange thing was there was no blood anywhere to be found, no footprints and no shredded clothes so that eliminated any chance of a wild animal attacking the kids. Sara immediately thought of that woman, who had lost her baby to a dingo, but of course the boys were far too big and that would not have been possible with their dogs there, who had been trained to attack anyone who came near the kids. Also, the tent was zipped up tight when they arrived back in camp. So, there was no explanation whatsoever to where the children and dogs could have gone.

In the morning the head of the settlement and two elders met with the frantic parents.

"What's wrong?" he asked.

"Our kids have disappeared, so have our guard dogs" George said while trying to hold back tears. "When we got back last night Sara went in to check on them and they were gone."

"I am sorry to hear that," the man said. Although the response, Sara thought was cold and unemotional, the man was genuinely concerned. He turned to one of the villagers and told him to run back to the village camp and send the men out to search. "We know the bush better than anyone. If they are out there my boys will find them."

While the males from the Aboriginal camp were out looking, George and Sara were too, even going to the extent of checking behind every rock and scouring every bush and shrub in the area. Terrifyingly, there was absolutely no sign of the kids and no footprints other than that of the adults. It was all too much, suddenly Sara broke down and fell on her knees crying and screaming that she wanted her kids back.

Hours later, just before sunset, the elders returned with the scary news they had found nothing. Desperate to find his kids, George got into his car and headed off to the nearest town 200 kilometers away.

A couple of hours later, he returned with the Northern Territory State Police. They spoke with Sara, the settlement's aboriginal elders, as well as all the local aboriginals. After everyone gave them their statements, the police spent several hours searching the area on foot and with their own search dogs. Even after all that still no trace of the kids or dogs was found.

The nest day the police returned again this time not only with the dogs, but with four wheel drives, motorbikes and a helicopter, but once again nothing was found.

One officer, a sergeant, took Sara aside and began asking questions again "Mrs. Towner, exactly where were you when your husband was with the men at the ceremony, were you with the children?" he asked.

"No," Sara replied. "I already told you all that I went with my husband; we knew the children would be safe as we left our dogs to guard them. They have been trained to immediately attack any strangers if they come near the children's tent. Then, while George was attending the initiation ceremony with the men away from the village, I was taken to spend time with the women. I was with the women until my husband came back. I never went anywhere."

The officer had a strange look on his face for just a second, as if he thought something was wrong. "Mrs. Turner, it's not the custom to leave children alone in the bush with only dogs for protection, also I never asked you, if you went anywhere," he said. "Why would you say to me, you never went anywhere?" Sara didn't, couldn't answer she was far too upset, and she was devastated that she had been so foolish to leave the children alone with the dogs, but she also wondered, why all these questions, everyone knew she loved her kids more than life itself.

"Are you done with my wife," George asked angrily. "I would like to look some more for my kids if you don't mind!" He wasn't feeling in control of the situation at all, he was not himself. He had such fear and anger deep within him, and right at that moment he didn't know where to aim it.

"Mr. Turner, I am finished for now, but there may be more questions we need answered later," the officer stated. Then he inquired how long they would be staying in the area. George told him until the kids were found, then he added that if no answers were coming forth soon from the Northern Territory Police as to where the boys were or what had happened to them, then, possibly they would be heading back to Sydney to raise funds to seek private assistance.

"Well, I will try to be back in the next few days, please be here when I do Mr. Turner, as I probably will have a lot more questions to ask if your kids are still missing." Then he and the rest of the police got back into their cars and drove back to town.

Sara and George spent the rest of the day going over every area they had already covered, looking for some kind of clue to what could have happened. But it leads to the same result, nothing absolutely nothing. They were so distraught; they even refused the food that the aborigines had kindly prepared for them. One of their religious leaders did come over and bless the site, as well as George. "This will keep you safe from the evil spirits who wander the bush," he said. For some reason he did not issue a blessing to Sara. He just turned his back on her and walked away. George called to him to come back, but the man just kept on walking back to the camp settlement.

The sun was down by this time and for some reason George was having trouble getting a fire started so they decided to get some much needed rest. Neither of them fell asleep right away. Between their hunger and worry for their kids, sleep would just not come. Finally, just as the moon hit its apex, they both fell asleep. It wasn't restful, but it was sleep.

Sometime during the night a wind kicked up, blowing in from the north. The sound of the tent rattling in the wind woke Sara. "George," she said in a whisper as she shook him. "George, wake up."

"What is it Sara?" George said as his eyes opened.

"Listen," she said with a tone of hope in her voice. He strained his ears and could only hear the wind blowing. "Listen, I can hear the kids. I can hear them calling for me. They want their mum... they want their mum." She was in tears as she spoke. "Their voices are so sad, so lonely. They need me George... they need their mum." She ran out of the tent, still in her nightgown, and ran off into the bush.

"Sara," George yelled as he watched her run off. "Sara, come back here!" In seconds she was beyond his voice, and he could not find her. Afraid he would get lost and be no use to Sara or the kids, he returned to the campsite and just walked around the area calling for Sara and the kids, and made sure he kept the fire well lit. Maybe Sara, or even the kids, would see it and find their way back.

Sara made it back to the camp a couple of hours later. She was cut up and bleeding, but other than that, she was tired and hungry but she was okay. "I heard them," she said. "I really did. I swear on my life I heard them calling for me. I just kept walking and walking but I could not find them. I tried darling, I really did. I want my boys back."

"I know, honey," George said. "Let me put you to bed and bandage you up. If the boys do not return in the next 24 hours we will leave here and go into town and try to get some more help." Sara was scared to leave the campsite, but she agreed and fell asleep without any argument. She slept the entire day and night, she was so depressed and exhausted, even so she would wake every hour and urgently ask if the kids were back. George would just shake his head and go over and hold her hand gently until she fell back to sleep, as the tears rolled down his face. He felt so guilty, why had he ever agreed to go to the ceremony. He also could not help thinking that Sara had touched the Bullroarer maybe that was why; maybe the evil spirits had stolen their children.

The next day, once Sara woke up, they spent hours searching for the kids, before they realized they needed professional help. So they packed their stuff, let the tribal leaders know that they were leaving and where they would be if the boys should possibly return, and then they made their way to Oooawonga... the next closest town. They went to a small local hotel and checked in. The hotel was a real dump and the hotel room smelt of urine, but they did not care, all they wanted to do was find their kids. Once they unpacked George and Sara went out into the street to go to the state police office.

As soon as they stepped out of the door Sara noticed that every eye, they passed was on her. The looks ranged from pity to anger and hatred. A few people even crossed the street so they would not have to even pass by her. "The rumors have started," George said in a faint whisper. "They remember that other woman and her missing baby." Sara didn't say anything; she just kept walking and staring straight ahead. Finally, she snapped.

"I didn't do anything!" she screamed. "I fucking love my kids. I would never, ever hurt them!" By now the entire town had them surrounded. They were not even looking at George. Their anger was aimed at Sara and no matter what George said there was nothing he could do about it except to hurry Sara into the police station.

"Did you find them?" the sergeant asked as they rushed in. Of course they answered no...the kids were still missing. He asked them a few more questions, gave them some food and some advice that he strongly recommended that they follow. "Go back to the hotel, get your car and get out of town," he said. "Leave what you have unpacked in the room and just get the hell out of town now! Please do not delay, go now!" He emphasized the word "now." "It is for your own good. Honestly, it is.

We will keep looking for your children and notify you immediately if we find them. I must admit though, that does not look like it is going to happen. We can find no trace of them at all. This has never happened before; usually there is always some sort of clue. I am so very, very sorry! The whole town is in an uproar, I strongly advise you to go now."

"What about our stuff?" George asked.

"I will personally pack it up and send it to you," the officer said. So George and Sara went outside under police escort, got in their car, and left.

It took four days to get back to real civilization, meaning they reached Brisbane. They spent a couple days there. The headlines in the newspaper were about the missing kids in the outback, but luckily, there were no pictures, except for pictures of the two boys, so Sara had no problems. Although all they wanted to do was rest… that never came to Sara. She didn't eat or sleep. She just cried the whole time and paced back and forth across the room. It was so bad that George had to fill her with pills to even get her to sit down. He had never seen her so distraught, and he decided he had to get her home as soon as possible, she needed help.

The next morning, before they began their journey back home, Sara asked George to do something for her. She wanted to travel the coast road to Sydney and on the way see the Gold Coast. "It's a beautiful place," she said. "I have heard so much about it. I really do want to see it George, maybe that will help calm me down a little!" Naturally, George agreed, and she spent the next half hour talking about the ocean and how beautiful she always thought it was. Happy that at least Sara was communicating instead of crying all the time, George set his GPS and they headed towards Sydney via the Gold Coast.

When they arrived at the famous Gold Coast resort Surfers Paradise, they decided to drive down Main Beach Parade, and after some searching they eventually found a place to park. As they did Sara saw a restaurant across the street. Smiling for the first time since that terrible night Sara asked George "Honey, could you please go over to that little restaurant and see if you can get me a salad, I think I really do need to eat something, I'm feeling a little faint!" Thrilled that, at long last, his wife wanted something to eat, George left her sitting on a bench admiring the ocean as he headed off to get her salad.

The service was very slow, and then suddenly George had a thought that made him rush back to his wife. As he made it over to the bench, George could not see Sara anywhere, then suddenly he saw her fully clothed, calmly walking out into the surf. The waves were bigger than normal, and soon the waves were smashing against Sara and she soon disappeared under them.

The Surfer's Paradise Lifeguards, and also George, began rushing out to her side, but by the time the lifeguards reached where Sara was last seen, there was no trace of her. The waves were just too strong and the currents were just too much for them to search for her more than a few minutes. They all agreed they would look for the body when the waves calmed a little and they could get more help. However, hours later, despite all of the help no body was ever found.

George stayed at the Gold Coast for over a week. He continued looking for Sara as well as filling out papers at the local police station, plus planning a funeral, if or when the body was found. It never was.

Eventually he drove back to Sydney by himself. It was hard, and there were more than a few times when he thought about driving off the side of a mountain road but he fought the urge. That would not be something that Sara would have ever wanted.

He made it back to their house sometime on Saturday night. It was rough. He could still hear the kids playing in their room and he could still smell the perfume that Sara always wore. It was a special blend that he had made for her so no one else in the world would ever smell the same as she did. Now their house, so filled with love and laughter, was silent. So silent, he wanted to scream, the pain was so unbearable... his sons, and now his wife, what had he done to deserve such hell?

Finally, after a few days he started unpacking his bags. Inside the first one he opened, he found a note. It was written by Sara. He opened it and immediately started crying. It said, "Darling George, I know that I have hurt you, and hurt you badly, forgive me my darling but I have to be with my children. They are calling me I can hear them. Please do not mourn for me or the boys. We will be happy and we will be waiting for you when you are ready... I love you my darling... your Sara." He grabbed the paper in both hands and tore it to shreds then he spent the night drinking Jack Daniels and beer and crying. He knew this was not something Sara would have wanted, though he still could not accept she had abandoned him. He loved her, he needed her, and he needed the boys. Why did she do this? After a few days of deep sorrow, he decided to get on with life. Yes, he was desperately hurt and sad, but he also knew that Sara had loved him and would have wanted him to go on living.

The next morning he went back to work as if nothing had happened. There were a lot of questions that he didn't want to answer, but everyone was cool about it and they realized that he would talk when he wanted to and not a minute before, so the questions stopped.

That night he went home to an empty house. He started to unpack his other bag and in it found the bullroarer. As he looked at it, he remembered the leader of the village telling him, under no conditions was a woman ever to touch it. Sara had been warned so many times it was for men only. George had told her more than once not to touch it, but she did, and look what happened. All of a sudden George's anger grew to a point where he could control it no longer. grabbed the bullroarer and slammed it across his knee, splitting in half. Then he spent a very, very long time breaking it into smaller and smaller pieces. Once each piece was no more than splinters he sat down, drank a whole bottle of Jack and finally passed out.

    The next morning George was awakened by loud knocking on the door. "It's the police," a loud voice said from the other side. "Could you please open the door? I have to talk to you." George knew that voice. It was the officer from that little town.

    "Just a minute," he yelled as he grabbed his pants. His thoughts were running wild about what they would say. He quickly got his pants on and rushed to the door. When he opened it, he was not only the cop from the town, but the head of the village was there with him.

    "Is Mrs. Towner here with you?" the man asked. "We would like to talk to her too." George told them what had happened. They expressed their sympathies, but then hurriedly went on. "Mr. Towner… we have good news. We found your children last night. They were up by Uluru."

    "Ayres Rock," George said. "That was…"

    "325 kilometers from where you were camped," the tribal leader said with a smile. "No one knows how they got there, but they were found tired and hungry. Some people there took them in and helped them until the word spread and the people realized who they were. They called the police, and we have your kids with us now."

    "Where are they," George asked as his excitement grew. "Where are they?"

    The officer beckoned to a second policeman waiting outside in a police car, he got out opened the back door of the car, and within seconds George's sons were running towards their father. They were wrapped in blankets and outfits of brand new clothes. "Dad," they both yelled in unison. They ran up and did something those boys stopped doing years before. They both ran up and gave George so many hugs and kisses. When he questioned them about what had happened, they could not tell George what had happened to them, or where the dogs had gone as they honestly remembered nothing.

As soon as he had put the boys to bed, George, the officer and the village leader sat on the couch. They all talked, trying to figure things out and then George admitted that Sara had touched the bullroarer.

The Aboriginal elder looked shaken and sad. Then he reminded George what he had said. "Where is the bullroarer now," he asked. George pointed to a pile of wood shards in the corner of the room. No one said a word until the village leader asked when he smashed it.

"Last night," George said.

"Then the curse has been broken," the village leader said as he and the police officer prepared to leave the house. "We will leave you now to live your life." Then he told George to be respectful of the wood shards and to be careful where he disposed of them.

George still lives in the same house with his two boys, who have grown like weeds. They still cannot remember or explain how they suddenly found themselves at Uluru, or how they got there, or what happened to their dogs. They just accept the fact it happened. George makes sure he always tells them of their mother and makes sure that they know just how much she loved them. He also tells them the story of the bullroarer. They don't of course believe in that kind of stuff, but it does make for a good story... doesn't it???

The Attack of the Killer Cassowaries

As Americans, we should have known better, but naturally as avid bird watchers wanting a unique new experience, nothing was going to stop us. A level five storm hit Australia in the area along the Queensland coast and we heard that going into the bush in Australia after a major storm like that was more than perfect for avid bird watchers to find some of the unique Australian birds who were usually hidden from view by the thick vegetation. The thing was, no one warned us about exactly what we would find!

After an airline flight of more than thirty hours we ended up in Cairns, a big tourist resort which typhoon Yasi had not hit like other areas, even though before the hurricane it had been issued a warning of evacuation.

Upon arrival in Cairns, we decided to spend the night there and found a fairly nice motel. It wasn't big or fancy, but it had everything we needed, including a Maccas nearby, and an RSL Club with what Australians call pokies, so despite the chaos of the storm we had it made. Plus, there were some pretty hot girls hanging around the Hotel, so that made it even better.

We rested for a couple of hours and then went out to get something to eat. That meant a bunch of Quarter Pounders and chips but we decided to take the food back to the room. Of course, we needed something to drink, so I went over to buy a case of Australia beer, naturally I asked for Fosters, but apparently all those ads in the States were just sucking us in, Fosters was not on the menu no way, no how! We ate in our room, and then had a couple of drinks downstairs with some pretty Aussie girls. After that we all went over to the RSL club, where I won 300 bucks, and then we went back to the Hotel and, after wasting my time on a hot Aussie tease, I went to bed solo.

Now, there was a lot of destruction all over the place. It was actually very depressing, but we tried to put that in the back of our mind and, in the morning, started out for a place where we guessed that we might find what we were looking for. Half of the roads we tried driving on were flooded and impassable, so what should have been a short drive took us all day. Eventually we found ourselves in Japoon National Park.

Due to the storm some locals had set up free food along the side of the road. I had never met such friendly people. We sat and talked with them over tea, steak, and sausages, which they called snags. I told them where we were going, and what we were looking for, and almost immediately their tone changed.

"You do not want to do that," one of them told us. "People have been seriously hurt going into the Park after a storm." I asked why, but they either wouldn't or couldn't tell us anything except that everything that we had heard about sighting rare birds was a whole lot of rubbish and we were being conned by Australian tourism bullshit. Then they left us while they attended to a couple who had lost everything in the storm.

After they had taken care of the young couple, one of our hosts returned to chat with me, while my fellow bird watching companions were busy chatting up a couple of young well-endowed birds on horseback.

"Mate, if you come all this way go ahead, don't take our word for it and stick to the main tracks in the area, I reckon' she'll be right, but it's a real bastard if you get off the beaten track. Make bloody sure you watch out for them cassowaries, they are real bastards. Still, I reckon after a storm they ain't the only mangy bastards around, there are bloody snakes, bloody crocs, dingoes, ticks and bloody mozzies galore."

I thanked him for the warning and got back in our rented SUV; my three friends reluctantly stopped chatting up the two females and joined me.

We decided to go as far as the road would take us... which ended up being only about twenty kilometers... many times we nearly found ourselves stuck in the mud, but luckily my friend Pete was an excellent navigator under catastrophic conditions. Eventually we found a small, cheap motel and made plans for the walk the next day.

There was a trail not too far from the motel so, in the morning, we started walking. It was headed toward one of the mountains in the area. The guy at the motel told us that the trail ended up at Dingo Mountain. It was well known as a place where a whole lot of rare animals and birds gathered. One thing for sure we never anticipated what we would find. At first it was just lizards and some small rodents but, then as we crossed a small clearing, suddenly thousands of crows, parrots, lorikeets, and cockatoos started screaming like hell. It was so loud that none of us could even think much less talk to each other.

We decided to set up camp, despite the noise. The area was surrounded by gum and bottle brush so we had a lot of fallen wood for a fire; unfortunately it was too wet, so eventually we found some discarded wood in a nearby cave. We spent the next hour or so setting up our tents, making a fire, then preparing and cooking a rabbit which Pete had shot when we first started looking for wood. The rabbit stew Mike cooked us was delicious. We ate, drank and laughed for quite a while and then we settled in for the night... all except Mike... he wanted to stay awake and check out the area at night. We watched through the tent flap as the light from his flashlight faded into the distance. I thought that he should have stayed in camp since he had quite a buzz on, but I was far too tired to try and stop him.

The sun rose early, and the Australian sun can be rough. It was hot, and the air was so humid that it was hard to breathe, but it looked like it was going to be a nice day.

Mike was lying outside of his tent. We thought that he must have passed out when he got back from his walk, so as we wanted an early start we went over and tried to wake him up. I shook him and his eyes opened and he let out a moan as he stretched out. It was then that we saw that he had several bruises on his head, arms, legs and chest. They were big and very dark in color.

"What in the hell happened to you," I asked as he started to sit up.

His voice was weak and shaky, but he did his best to explain all that had happened. "I was about a mile from here," he said. "I was just walking when something hit me from behind. I couldn't get my bearings and whatever it was just kept hitting me again and again. I tried to run, but when I turned there was another and another. Pretty soon they were all attacking me. I finally lost my footing and, as soon as I hit the ground, whatever they were they left, which was lucky, as I know I certainly would not be alive now, if it wasn't for me falling!"

"What were they," we asked.

"I don't know it was so dark. I swear I was being attacked from all sides, I am pretty sure they were some kind of giant birds. Fellas, I swear on my mother's grave I really thought I was going to die out there, how I managed to get back here I don't know. He was really upset, and we were sincerely sorry for him it was obvious he had been hurt very badly, the bruises were horrific; even so we couldn't help but smile a little. Mike, though a highly respected bird watcher, was actually terrified of any type of large bird.

Attacked by giant birds, no doubt he was so drunk, he must have fallen bumped his head and got caught in a fallen tree or something and some birds clustered round to take a look. Now we knew there were cassowaries in the area. After all, we had come all the way from America to spot, if we could, such rare birds as the Night Parrot, Sooty Tern and Long-billed Corellas, as well as Australia's popular Cockatoos, Kookaburras, Emus, and Wedge-tailed Eagles.

We all knew Mike was always a little inclined to exaggerate everything, and big birds gathering together and causing that kind of injury seemed a little too far-fetched. Mike had gone to clean up and when he came back, he must have heard us talking as he limped over and sat down on a log. "I see you guys don't believe me, but I swear they were some kind of big vicious birds. I remember reading once that cassowaries can be real killers, but I never believed it, not till now, but laugh all you like, I tell you guys I have never been so scared shitless in all my life."

Out of respect for Mike, for it was obvious he was beat up bad, Pete, Frank and I decided that we'd go and see if we could find exactly what had happened, so we asked Mike in what direction he had gone, and we took off... leaving him alone in the camp to rest.

About a mile in the direction he told us to go we found a clearing. The forest around that area was completely silent. It was so quiet the only we could hear were our hearts beating. Looking around the ground and the leaves were torn up. It did look like there had been a fight there recently. Maybe he was jumped by men who lived in the forest, or maybe not, but whatever happened, he had certainly gotten the shit beat out of him.

We didn't stay long in the clearing. We checked the area. It was surprising how messed up the area was. Then we saw something in a small patch of ground. It was a large, very large, footprint. It had three toes with a claw on the end of each one.

I wasn't exactly sure, but possibly it was the footprint of a cassowary, an ostrich, or an emu. Then I remembered yet another warning, we had seen in America on one of the local news shows... just before we left the States. You know the type of exaggerated tabloid news one cannot be really sure of. "The government is warning the residents of the areas affected by the latest storm in Queensland, Australia, to avoid any contact with cassowaries," the announcer said. "Food shortages have caused aggressive behavior with the birds, and they are capable of killing a human being with their claws."

"Oh my God," I yelled. "Let's get back to camp, maybe Mike was right, maybe it was a cassowary attack. We have to get back!" I grabbed my two friends and we hurriedly made our way to camp site. We made it in about ten minutes and once we entered the campsite we saw Mike lying on the ground near where he had been sitting. He wasn't moving and he was face down in the dirt. I went over and rolled him onto his back. There was blood all over him, and we could see deep gashes covering his chest and abdomen. It looked as if he was a prop in some very bad horror film but this was real.

Then we noticed that all of the birds and animals we had heard the day before were gone. There was not a noise coming from the bush except some leaves shuffling and twigs breaking. There was a feeling that we all shared that something was watching us and the brief sparks of red between the green leaves didn't do much to calm our fears.

"We had better get out of here," I said as my eyes darted around. "We'll send the authorities back to get him." Then we took a quick minute to say a few words and cover his body with leaves. None of us knew why, but it just seemed the right thing to do.

There were several paths out of the clearing. The problem was the three of us could not remember which one we took to get there but that didn't matter all we knew was we needed to get the hell out of there. Down each of the paths we could hear large animals running through the forest. Then came the screams. They were loud and they sounded like whatever those things were they were talking to each other. That made our imaginations switch into overdrive. The last time we heard sounds like that it was in a really bad sci-fi movie. They were the noises Velociraptors made when they were planning to attack humans when they got to close to their nests.

"What in the hell is that?" Fred asked, but before I had the chance to say anything, a large vicious angry bird came running toward us. It had to have been doing at least twenty-five miles an hour. I know it was at least that much because it just clipped me on the shoulder and I felt as if I had been hit by a truck.

After I regained my senses, I looked at Pete and Frank. They must have been hit harder than I was. They were lying crumpled up against a tree at the other end of the clearing. They were both... bruised and battered but okay for the most part, but, the minute Frank stood up, the cassowary came back through the clearing... hitting him from behind. This time he flew head first into the ground and he didn't get back up. His eyes were flickering as I walked across to him.

"What was that?" he asked in a weak, broken voice.

"I think that was one of those cassowaries the news was talking about," I said. As I said that, the bird came running back, and it kicked Frank in the head with its claws. I saw his skull shatter and his blood start to pour out, then it headed over to Pete and attacked him just as hard, and I knew he had also killed Pete. Before I had the chance to react, the bird ran to the edge of the clearing, turned to look at me and I swear to God that it was laughing at what it did. Then the noise got louder as the rest of the cassowaries who were hiding in the forest started to laugh with it.

"You son of a bitch," I yelled as the bird turned and looked at me. I moved slowly but with determination, reaching down and picking up a stick which was at my feet. As I rose my anger grew replacing any fear that I may have had. "C'mon, why not me? Why don't you come after me?"

The bird just looked at me, and then it suddenly let out the most Godforsaken screech I had ever heard. Then it started moving toward me. It wasn't moving fast, but it was steady. As it walked closer I kept my eyes locked on it. There was anger. I could see it raging deep within the bird's soul. It wanted to kill me, and I had no understanding why.

"C'mon," I yelled again. I raised the stick above my head and stood as tall and I could, bringing my shoulders back and throwing my chest out. I knew from TV that if you are facing down a wild animal you should make yourself as big as possible to show dominance. As it moved even closer I braced myself on my back foot and locked myself into a fighting stance. Finally it got to within a few feet of me. I was watching every move that it made, every breath, it took, and I swear I was listening to its heart beating but I didn't move.

I watched as it right foot came off of the ground and, as soon as it did, I swung my stick hitting the bird in the side of its long neck. It lets out a scream, but it was not the same sound it had made earlier. This time it was in pain; I had hurt it, and hurt it badly. Still, it didn't fall. It quickly regained its composure and took a vicious swipe at me with its beak, it made contact and I could feel warm blood, my blood running down my face and onto my chest. "Mother fu...," I yelled as it braced itself for another swipe. I saw it, take its head and start the swing while, at the same time, raising its leg to attack with its claws.

I swung the stick once again and once again I hit the bird in the side of the neck but this time it was different. I heard and loud crack and I felt its neck shatter beneath the force of the wood. It dropped to the ground and blood poured from its mouth and eyes. As soon as it hit the ground the forest went silent and twenty or more cassowaries stepped from the surrounding trees.

"Oh shit," I said under my breath. At that moment I was afraid, more afraid than I had ever been. I was surrounded by birds that I had seen kill already and I was just standing there with a stick in my hand and the body of a dead cassowary on the ground at my feet.

I watched as they began circling me... moving a little closer with every step they made. Finally, one of them turned and walked up to me. Its face was no farther than just a few inches from mine. The thing was, it didn't look angry or anything like that. It looked like a bird and that was all. I get up the nerve to smile at it and as I did it reached over and touched my forehead with the tip of its beak. I didn't know what to do or what it meant, but I knew somehow that it wasn't going to hurt me.

I started walking backwards toward the edge of the trees. I watched as, one by one, each of the Cassowaries walked over and started pecking at their fallen comrade. I didn't know what they were doing and, quite frankly, I didn't want to know, I just got my ass out of there.

The next morning I wandered into some small town. I didn't know the name of it and I didn't really care. I was alive and that was good enough.

I spent the next few days answering questions, being interviewed by the TV news and lastly taking representatives of the Game Council out to the site, so they could investigate the incident and arrange to bring the bodies back so they could be transferred back home to their families. I went with them to the site and got permission to travel back home to the States with the transported bodies of Mike, Pete and Fred, I'll be damned if I was going to leave my friends' bodies traveling alone on that plane like a delivery of frozen meats.

After that day, I never thought of going bird watching ever again, but I did return to Australia, but this time I stuck to the big cities, and I never went into the outback ever again as I, to

this day, remember those damn birds and how a storm cost my friends their lives even though it was long gone before we got there.
    If only we had listened!

An ANZAC Warrior In A Moment of Peace

My family moved from Canada to Australia way back around 1894. Before you ask.... No, they were not convicts! They migrated here because they decided that they loved the idea of warm tropical climate, a new country away from the six months of snow they had to suffer in Montreal every year. My great grandfather was the 1st Aussie born son to the Innis family a few years later in their new home town of Port Walcott.

Being a proud Australian, the moment he turned eighteen, my great grandfather, Daniel Innis, joined the army. He was assigned to the Australian and New Zealand Army Corps of the Mediterranean Expeditionary Force. In 1916 he was sent overseas to the Western Front where they fought a major battle with huge losses on both sides. Not only did they have to fight the enemy, the ANZACS also had to fight the cold, it was so cold if the German artillery did not get you, the cold probably did! It was so intense many men actually froze to death.

Now, according to a story that has been passed down from generation to generation for nearly one hundred years, great grandpa Innis was part of a machine gun unit. He obviously was a good soldier, and knew what he was doing and it was rumored he killed more than two hundred of the enemy and took even more prisoner.

Now, it wasn't that he hated Germans. He didn't hate anyone; neither did his parents who for those early days in Australia were very liberal thinkers.

Young Daniel had grown up with a mixture of Aussie immigrants from all over the world, Germans, Italian, Irish, Asian and even quite a few local Aboriginal kids, which was really unheard of in that era. His parents held regular bush barbies with a whole mixture of folks and surprisingly, with all of the beer and plonk they drank at those barbies… they never had any major blues, although it was said some of the discussions, especially when it got round to politics, did get quite heated and sometimes maybe a beer bottle or two was broken over someone's head, but despite it all, everyone always left as friends.

Naturally, when the war broke out, and when their son was shipped to the Western Front, Daniel's parents, being dinkum Aussie patriots, took genuine pride in the fact their son was overseas fighting the bloody Krauts.

In the Somme, towards the end of a major skirmish, great grandpa Daniel was shot, soon after he had saved the lives of ten men in his battalion by single handedly killing 5 Germans firing in their direction, and then carrying all his wounded fellow ANZAC's to safety. Then another German fired and Daniel was wounded, luckily the wound wasn't too bad, but bad enough to take him out of the action. Unfortunately, by then his battalion had retreated to the other side of a small hill and, when he eventually opened his eyes, to his horror he found himself face to face with a German officer who was holding a rifle no more than a foot from his chest.

"I am Lieutenant Zaire Paul Hannig," the German officer said in perfect English, and still holding his rifle, he knelt down next to my great grandfather.

Great grandpa raised his hands as best he could. " I am Sergeant Daniel Innis, of the Australian and New Zealand Army Corps." Then, much to my great grandpa's amazement, the German officer raised his hand and saluted my great grandfather. Confused and also in deep pain from his wound, my great grandfather just looked at Lieutenant Hannig knowing full well at any moment he was about to die.

"Sergeant Innis," Hannig said with a strange look on his face. "Do not be afraid, I may be a Kraut, but I was educated in England and many of my friends were British soldiers. You may not believe this, but I have killed far too many in a war I do not believe in... I am tired of all of this death and blood and I want no more of it. A few hours ago I shot yet another young British soldier. I watched him die a painful death. He did not deserve to die, especially because of me. No, I tell you I want no more of this killing, I refuse to ever kill again, so here and now I wish to surrender to you!" Then Lieutenant Hannig took his rifle and handed it to my great grandfather.

As he did, they both heard voices coming from behind them, and the voices were not speaking English. Aware that his unit was getting closer and closer, quietly, Hannig took off his shirt, starting tearing it in pieces and bandaged great grandpa's wounds. Apparently my Great grandfather had lost a lot of blood, but he was still conscious and he accepted the German's surrender by taking the offered rifle and gesturing with the rifle which way the allied forces were.

Lieutenant Hannig then picked up Great grandpa on his back, and he started toward the Anzac trenches... not knowing what kind of reception he was going to face. It was only a couple of miles, but throughout the entire journey they heard bullets buzzing around them and shells exploding closer that either of them were hoping for. Somehow they made it to within 20 meters of the Anzac line. Hannig put my great grandfather on the ground and walked toward the allied troops with his arms in the air. "I surrender, I surrender," he yelled as he walked closer. A number of the allies pointed their rifles and leveled them right at Hannig's heart. Great grandpa heard several of the hammers click into the ready position and he also heard some of the soldiers yelling for them to fire.

Great grandpa wasn't going to allow that to happen so he crawled between the Anzacs and Hannig. Hand over hand, he lifted himself to a position directly in front of Hannig as one of the soldiers fired... striking great grandpa in the shoulder. As he fell more than a dozen Anzacs ran forward and picked him up off of the ground. "Do not harm this man," great grandpa yelled. "He is not the enemy, he surrendered to me voluntarily, and he is my prisoner! He risked all to save my life." My grandpa Daniel was immediately rushed by the medics into a medical tent where his wounds were treated, except for the one in his shoulder, which was so severe that it cost him his arm, and that nearly cost him his life from a severe infection that set in soon after the surgery.

Hannig was immediately grabbed and taken to the Lieutenant Colonel. He was questioned rather intensely, but he was never harmed or tortured. After that he was eventually sent to the Knockaloe POW camp on the Isle of Man, where he spent the rest of the war.

Like I said, the story about Grandpa Daniel and Lieutenant Hannig has been told and retold over and over again, but the thing was there was never any proof that it really happened. I mean, yes, my great grandpa was a hero, and he did have the great honor of receiving The Victoria Cross for his gallant acts of bravery on the battlefield, and yes, he was missing an arm, but it was still just so hard to believe the stories about him saving a German officer's life. That was until a couple of weeks ago.

I was working in the garden in front of my house when a cheap rental car pulled into my driveway. "Are you Peter Innis?" a woman asked as she stepped out of the car. She was about the same age as I am and she had a thick German accent that I had trouble understanding. I told her that yes. I was indeed Peter Innis. "I am looking for a descendent of Sergeant Daniel Innis of the Australian Army."

"Well, I guess that would be me," I said.

She looked at me and smiled. "I always thought that story was just something they always told us," she said. I asked her what story, and immediately she started to tell me, the same story I had heard all of my life.

"My father died last year," she explained. "And when I was going through the attic, papers, I found an extremely large box with Sgt. Daniel Innis engraved on a metal plate." She then smiled "The box is very big, if you do not mind coming out to my car" We went out to her car and she opened her truck there was this very large wooden box. It was very old, and my great grandpa's name was inscribed on a metal plate.

Once again she smiled and with her thick accent stated "Apparently my great grandfather tried to find your great grandfather, as he had been entrusted with the delivery of this box, but unfortunately your great grandfather could not be traced and of course, there was no Internet in those days, and no War Memorial in Canberra to trace him either. They were so helpful, that is how I found you."

I did not know quite what to say as I carried this large old box back into the house.

"What is this?" I asked as I opened the box, which contained a very large magnificent sword.

"It is the Grosse Degen Imperial Sword," she said. Then I saw that there was a piece of paper lying beside the sword. I took it out, looked at it and asked her to translate it for me. "It says, 'I Friedrich Ebert, President, Republic of Germany do hereby award the Grosse Degen Imperial Sword to Sergeant Daniel Innis for honorably risking his own life to save the life of a German Officer."

The sword was truly magnificent, featuring an intricate floral pattern decoration in brass, with raised motifs all over the guard and pommel. Even though the grip end was decorated with elaborate floral chasing, it must have weighed at least two and a half kilos, and the blade also had delicate, raised, floral designs on both sides. I was indeed quite stunned, and I did not quite know what to say, so I stated, "On behalf of my great-grandfather, I thank you for bringing this to me," as I placed the sword back in its scabbard. I was so overwhelmed and so proud. My great-grandpa was a hero, and he had, despite all he had done for his own country during World War 1, also risked his own life to save the enemy's life... and so, strangely enough, did the enemy save his life, ironic but true.

Fraulein Helga and I spoke for the next few hours. We talked about our families, our lives and a whole lot more about our great grandfathers, Then, it was time for her to return to Germany, so I took the sword out of the box again and placed it in a place of honor... on the mantelpiece with the Victoria Cross and great grandpa's picture placed in front of this large imposing sword, and there it is going to stay.

Yes, we have Remembrance Day and Anzac Day, where we pay our respects to all our fallen heroes, but life is never just about the good guys and the bad guys. That German sword, sitting beside the Victoria Cross on the mantelpiece, always reminds me. War should be unnecessary. What we all need to do is understand each other better and be united in caring for one another, living productive and peaceful lives.

Ned Kelly, Hangman's Noose

I thought I was smart, but I learned one important thing when I bought a business in Australia: always check the history of the building and/or property before entering discussions to make the purchase. I wish someone had told me that when I bought a property in Glenrowan, Victoria.

I never read history, and until the day I bought my house and started my small business, I really couldn't have cared less about it... another big mistake. It appears that the property I purchased was located on the property line of the old Glenrowan Inn. I have now discovered that the Glenrowan Inn had been the site of one of the best known, and most controversial, events in Australian history... the siege and shootout between police and a bush-ranger named Ned Kelly and his gang in 1880.

I purchased the house for a reasonably good price. It was a three-bedroom brick house with a fine fireplace, separate living and dining room, a lovely, large, old-fashioned kitchen, and three acres of land. I really expected to pay about $450,000, but the house was a steal at $230,000....I thought it was a deal too good to pass up, so I even paid in cash for the place. That was about a month before I actually moved from Melbourne. Yes, I had a lovely house there and had made some good friends, but I needed something new and a change from another cosmopolitan Australian city. Glenrowan seemed to offer just what I was looking for, so it was an easy decision.

The first day after I moved in, I have to admit that I was exhausted, but I still had work to do. The house was full of dust and feathers. Some of the windows were broken, and I replaced them so that the hot air would stay out, but even with that, it was still roasting when I went to bed.

That first night wasn't as quiet as I hoped it would be. Between the crows squawking and the neighborhood dogs howling their freaking heads off, it was almost impossible to fall asleep, but I did sometime around two in the morning, but that didn't last long. Suddenly, I heard the sounds of gunshots coming from outside. I decided not to go out to investigate, as I was new to the neighbourhood. It was probably some angry neighbor shooting at those damn birds or dogs, and I certainly did not want to get hit by mistake, so I just stayed in my bed and let whoever it was do whatever it was they were doing. I was happy as long as it didn't involve me, and it sure seemed to quiet the dogs. The next night, and the next, and the next were the same. Gunshots echoed through my house, but whatever it was, I now also started hearing lots of men talking, yelling, and crying mixed in with a lot of other weird noises.

At first, I had thought it was the neighbor shooting at the dogs. Still, on the second night I then thought that maybe it was just a bunch of Australian rednecks letting off steam. Still, I soon realized those voices weren't celebrating or even happy; they were full of hatred, anger, and fear, and I had a strong feeling by then that it was more than just a few people - in fact, it sounded like something severe was happening.

When the shooting started that night I got up off of my couch and went outside. There was a thick area of bushes between me and where the sounds were coming from, but as I wanted to see what was going on, I went into the scrub. It was about 500 meters of dense bushes, and so it took me a while to get through, but once I did, I found a fairly large corkwood tree, which was big enough for me to hide behind while I watched what was going on.

There was a building... I guess you could call it a building. The walls seemed to be there, but I couldn't see what was inside. However, I could see through the walls to the trees on the other side of the clearing. In front of the building, I saw a vast crowd of men. Most of them were crouched down with rifles and shotguns aimed at the front door of the building, and they were firing one shot after another.

"What's going on?" I asked myself. Then I heard a voice coming from beside me.

"Stay down," I was ordered. When I looked up, I saw an Australian soldier standing beside me. He had his shotgun pointed at the back of the building. "By God, I hope he comes this way... I really do." He stated

"Who?" I asked.

"Who do you think?" he said with shock in his voice. "That bastard flamin' Bank Robber is askin' for it! I'll admit he has taken a whole lot of people as hostages, but even so, we have finally got the bloody bastard cornered, and this time I swear he is not getting away!"

Once again, I asked who was cornered. "That son of a whore bastard Ned Kelly, of course," he replied impatiently. "Thank the Lord; at long last, we've finally got him!"

Then I watched as a man, dressed in what I would call only some sort of tin armour, stepped out on the inn's porch and opened fire on the officers. More than a few of them dropped after being shot, but for every shot the man made, the officers fired four times as many. No matter how many times the man was hit, he didn't go down; he just turned and walked back into the Glenrowan Inn.

"That was that bloody bastard scourge Kelly," the officer said as he started to level his gun and shoot at the building. "Bloody mongrel bastard," he stated angrily, "this time he has no chance, as I said, this time we'll get him."

It was about half an hour later. The shooting continued back and forth; in fact, it had been going off and on since that strange figure, with the square tin-plated armor over his head, had retreated into the building.

My watch said that it was 5:00 AM when a figure ran out from the back of the building. The soldier was still standing there beside me, and immediately, along with several other officers, he aimed carefully and fired.

Unfortunately, the shots missed, and the man continued to run. I will tell you, as that man in the tin armor started running, I had never heard such language from an officer of the law. But that morning, nothing was normal; it had been sheer pandemonium all night long.

"The bastard got away... he got away!" the officer screamed." I could have killed the bloody mongrel bastard, but I missed! How could I have missed?"

Immediately, several of the men, including the officer, ran into the bush in search of the man in armor, but within minutes, they returned.

Observing all this, I tried to stay calm. I didn't know if I could easily get killed in all of this chaos, but I did know one thing... I wasn't going to take the chance. I could not return to my house until all this was over.

"I didn't miss," he yelled. "I did hit him! We wounded him badly at long last, " he proudly stated. "Oh yes, he may have gotten away for now, even though there was blood pouring out from his wound, but that tricky bastard, I swear on my Mother's grave, that bastard is in for it now, he will not get away from me this time! I'll make sure of that!" he angrily stated.

He was very frustrated and angry, but as an officer, he was under orders. Despite his anger and frustration, he stayed at his post, watching and waiting. However, he didn't have to wait long.

A man was observed heading back into the house. The man was limping as he headed for the back door of the hotel.

Then, within a couple of minutes, I heard another round of gunshots coming from the hotel. This time, the battle lasted about fifteen minutes, and then there was silence.

The sun was getting high in the sky when I saw hostages start to walk out of the hotel and into the waiting arms of the surrounding police. For some reason, these outlaws had decided to release all the hostages.

I suppose they knew their time for robbing banks was over and that they might have an easier time of it if all the remaining hostages were released unharmed. I then heard somebody yell.

"We've captured Ned, he came down in a gully back behind the Hotel. We've got that flamin' bastard at long last! May he be hanged by the neck and his soul rot in hell forever."

At that moment, once the hostages were safe, the commander of the police raised his arm, and the officer who had stayed beside me ran out and joined several others, who lit some straw and set the Glenrowan Inn alight, hoping to flush out the few remaining Kelly gang members.

The moment the building was in flames, there were more gunshots, and Dan Kelly was apparently shot dead along with several other gang members.

Suddenly, all was deathly silent, except for the sounds of weeping from some of the freed female hostages, who had come to like their colourful captors, and now the entire Kelly gang in the Glenrowan Hotel were dead.

The officer I had been watching all night long suddenly, along with all of the others, faded slowly from view, and I was left looking at an empty field. The next thing I knew, I was once again back in my bed, but this time with a fired rifle by my side, and on the bedroom wall a copy of a painting of Ned Kelly in his metal armour by Russell Drysdale staring down at me.

The next morning, I visited the town hall and researched information about the Glenrowan Inn and Ned Kelly. The more I read, the more I realized that everything I had seen, everything I had experienced had really happened. I had seen the final stand of Ned Kelly. Then I read something that made me smile and confirmed what I had seen... Kelly had been brought down from a shotgun shot to the legs. He did it, I thought. That son of a bitch got Ned Kelly, and I was there to see it!

I also read that the neck had hanged Ned Kelly at the Melbourne jail for the murder of Constable Thomas Lonigan on November 11th, 1880. His last words were "Ah, well, I suppose it has to come to this. "Another version of what he said is "Such is life!"

You know, how I wished during those nightly experiences that Ned Kelly and I could have talked a little bit. He is one of the most controversial men in Australian history, and bloody hell, I didn't even get to say G'day.

Since then, the nights had been quiet, far too quiet, and I missed the gunshots and all that I had witnessed. After all, how many people get to experience history? I guess I was the lucky one that night!

However, the experience had left its mark, and a few weeks later, I decided to sell my business and head back to Melbourne. So, a few days after that, I went over to see my accountant and the real estate agent, and then headed over to the bank to transfer my account to their Melbourne branch. The Bank was closed, and on the door was a prominent notice.

This Bank, unfortunately, closed due to Bank Robbery by several men wearing tin-plated armour. URGENT: All local Ghost Hunters, please get in touch with Constable Thomas Lonigan Jr. A large reward is offered for any information or explanation regarding the current Bank Robberies in Glenrowan, Euroa, Wangaratta, Beechworth, and Jerilderie.

Killara

Amarina Janjula was a typical little Aboriginal girl living in the outback near Marla, South Australia. Before giving birth to Amarina, her parents had tried many times in the past to have a child, but the outcome was always the same... Amarina's mother would miscarry after a couple of months. Once the couple decided not to try for another child, they found that the spirits had once again blessed their union.

Happily, this time the pregnancy went full term, and Amarina was born on one of the few nights when a storm rolled across the country. The rain was stronger than anyone in the settlement could remember. Amarina's father watched as trees were ripped from the ground and thrown so far he couldn't see them anymore. The rain was so hard that it wasn't falling the way normal rain falls; it was shooting straight across the air. Amarina's dad was hit by such hard raindrops that he felt them cutting into his skin. The lightning was constant, and the thunder made their dwelling shake violently as it tried to remain intact.

In the middle of this storm, Amarina had come into the world. Her mother was crying with joy and pride. Suddenly, the baby let loose with her first cry and snuggled into her mother's soft, pillow-like breasts. The two proud parents and all their relatives were celebrating so hard that no one noticed a young dingo pip wandering into their dwelling seeking shelter from the storm. The pup was only about five weeks old and was so small that it was no wonder nobody noticed when it curled up beneath Amarina's parents' bed and fell asleep.

During that first night, Amarina slept soundly in her proud mother's arms, but every so often she would stir and start to cry loudly for five minutes or so and then, just as suddenly, fall peacefully back to sleep... Every time she awoke, the pup would prick up his ears and would not go back to sleep until the baby stopped crying. The storm had caused the pup to be separated from his mother. It was terrifying out there, but here it was nice and warm, and he suddenly knew that he was needed here by the spirits to protect this helpless little human baby. By her side was where he would always belong.

In the morning, the hunt once again was a hub of activity. People came and went throughout the day, but something unexpected occurred. Amarina was lying on a small blanket on the floor. Slowly, the dingo cub walked out from under the bed and walked over to the center of the floor. The people around him didn't faze him; he just walked over to where Amarina was sleeping and stood there, gazing down at her, and then gave a sniff of curiosity.

Even though it was a very young pup, the people in the room began shooing the dingo out of the hut. Suddenly, the young dingo pounced on Amarina's blanket, and a rat appeared from under the blanket. The dingo grabbed the rat in its mouth before it could attack the baby. The young dingo killed the rat, and then he went over and very gently licked the baby's cheek. Then the dingo pup looked at Amarina's mother and then her father, and then just lay down on the edge of the blanket beside Amarina and went back to sleep.

"Them dingo pup is something special," Amarina's father exclaimed. "He is a friend to our baby daughter, and I know that they will be one for all of time. We will call the pup Killara as he came to us out of the storm, and from now on, he will be part of our mob." As this statement was made, Killara looked up, gave a soft howl, and then put his head back down and once again went back to sleep.

As Amarina grew, she and Killara became closer and closer. It got so that if you saw Amarina, you knew Killara was no more than a few feet away. Killara would only eat the food that the little girl shared with him, and when Amarina went to bed, the dingo would sleep on the same mattress with his head right next to Amarina's.

Then the day came that was never to be forgotten by Amarina's parents. Their beautiful little girl was celebrating her fifth birthday with her family when all their lives changed forever. By federal law, children of that particular mob, due to a lack of any schooling, were to be taken to be educated at a faraway Mission and later sent to live with white families so that they would leave behind their traditional ways and assimilate into the Christian European society.

So, on that day, the man in charge went from hut to hut in the settlement looking for children and taking as many as he and his men could find. The sounds of screaming mothers and crying children were so loud that it was impossible to hear anything else.

Finally, he got to Amarina's parents' hut. Her parents had tried to hide their beloved little girl in an old crate behind the hut, but when the white fella showed up, they had a paper from the authorities saying that a five-year-old girl lived there, and they wanted her. "Where is she?" the man in charge ordered as he entered the hut. Amarina's mom and dad didn't say a word, but Killara, without knowing it, showed the officials exactly where she was.

The dingo ran out of the hut and sat on the crate, snapping at anyone who came near it. He was howling loudly and even tried to paw open the crate; he could not understand why his little mistress was in this human box, as this was the first time Amarina had ever been out of his sight, and he had no idea how to handle it.

The man in charge walked over, pushed the animal out of the way as the dingo snapped at him, and he hit Killara with a baton. Killara was thrown across the yard as the crate was opened, and little Amarina was found cowering in the corner of the box. She was terrified, and tears were running down her face. "Please don't take me," she said in a voice that showed a kind of sad panic that no child should ever have known, but that didn't make a difference... neither did the cries of Amarina's mother. The Government official reached in, grabbed Amarina by the arms, and lifted her. Amarina's mother reached for her daughter, but her husband pulled her back immediately.

"Don't," was all he said to her. He knew what those men were capable of. He had seen it before in other areas, and it could end with his wife in jail or killed as an anarchist against the crown's authority. Just as she had been told to do, she reluctantly backed down, but for Killara, it was a different matter.

He saw what was going on... his best friend... his beloved little mistress was being taken away, so it didn't take long for the manner he had always shown to disappear and for his dingo nature to come through. Without any warning, he charged with his teeth bared, and he buried them deeply into the man's leg. The official tossed Amarina to two other men, who took her and placed her into a waiting wagon. As the door closed and locked, Killara went on the attack again, going after every man who was wearing a uniform. They all scrambled and got into the moving wagon, but that didn't stop Killara. He chased the wagon down the road, jumping at the windows. He snapped at the wheels, barking and jumping on the back of the wagon... to no avail. The wagon just continued down the road.

Amarina's father felt so helpless as he watched the wagon driving away, and cried out in deep despair as his little precious daughter disappeared over the horizon. He knew there was nothing he could do about it; it was the evil law of the white fellas. However, he was thankful that Killara was following the wagon, and he knew nothing bad was going to happen to his little girl. He and his family may have lost their beautiful child, possibly forever, but at least she would always be safe if Killara were there looking out for her.

They did not keep Amarina in the Mission for very long; instead, she was sent to live with a white family in Adelaide. There were stories of a dog that sat outside the government mission where the children were taken. As Amarina had been taken away in the middle of the night, Killara was sleeping outside the mission gate and did not realize she had been taken far, far away. Everyone soon noticed the dog that sat outside the government mission where the children were taken. One day, he realised his little mistress must not be there, so for months, he searched the area for her, but eventually, even he realised she was nowhere to be found.

Finally, it was the middle of June when Killara returned home to Marla. The first thing he did was to check Amarina's hut to see if she had returned; of course, she was not there. Killara walked back and forth around the property, carefully checking every inch of it, where his little mistress had ever played. Once again, he was disappointed. Eventually, he was so heartbroken that he lay down at the side of the road near the tree where Amarina had carved her name with her mother and father just before her fifth birthday. His tail fell to the ground, and his whines could be heard throughout the bush.

Learning that Killara was back home, Amarina's parents came and took him back to their hut, but he would always run away and go back to the exact spot where he last saw that wagon by the tree where his little mistress had carved her name.

Day after day… night after night, that dingo sat in the same spot along the road. He kept looking down the road as if he were waiting for Amarina to return. He refused food or even water when it was offered and even snapped at a few people who tried to force-feed him or move him from his spot.

Two weeks later, after having brought Killara back to the hut numerous times only to have him run off back to the old white gum, Amarina's father went once again to check on Killara. He found his body lying on the side of the road. His eyes were open, and he was still watching down the road just as he had done for so long. The locals claimed the dingo had starved to death, but Amarina's parents knew that he had died of a broken heart... it was a death that the local Aboriginals wept over, as his death was such a reminder of the lost generation that all would never forget or be able to forgive

The Aboriginal elders honored the loyalty of the dingo cub who had come in out of the rain and shown such loyalty to one of their own, so they had a statue of him placed by the old white gum as a sign of respect. So now Killara still sits in that spot on the road by Amarina's white gum, and his eyes are still watching for his friend. If you listen very carefully, you can hear the wind blowing through the nearby gum tree, and it sounds just like a dingo whining.

A couple of decades later, a young woman stopped her car at the spot where she and her family had once lived. They were all gone... driven off by white industrialists and the police years ago. The young woman didn't stay long, but she didn't drive far either. She stopped at the statue by the side of the road. She didn't say a word. She just got out of the car, went over, and placed a collar around the statue's neck. Then she wrapped her arms around the chest of the animal and hugged it as tight as she could. "I love you, Killara," she finally whispered into the statue's ear. Then she walked over to the white gum and carefully carved Killara's name. Just then, a breeze blew through the gum tree, and she heard the howl she knew as a girl, and she knew that, wherever her friend was, Killara was now content, and for the first time in so many years, so was Amarina.

The story is still told and retold through the Aboriginal communities about the lost baby and the dingo pup, Killara. In recent years, due to the numerous stories told about the Stolen Generation and the belated apology given to Aboriginal people by the Australian Prime Minister, Amarina's and Killara's story has spread across the Australian continent. In fact, over the years, quite a few people have come from all over the world to visit the statue of the now famous dingo, Killara.

Forty years later, travelling from her home in Adelaide, Amarina once again came back to the land where she was born, and returned to visit Killara's statue by the side of the road. She brought her two young granddaughters, and their dingo cub Arallik, who sat there beside the statue patiently gazing into his two young mistresses' eyes with the same adoration that young Killara had for his little Amarina so many years before... As they stood there, the young dingo cub suddenly gave a loud howl as if he was calling to someone, and at that moment, the wind started blowing through the old white gum, and it sounded just like a dingo howl of approval and inner peace.

About The Author

R.E. Taylor has been traveling throughout Australia for more than a year now. The more he met people and learnt about the non-tourist legends that circulate through the country, the more his imagination was stimulated to record his version of these incredible yarns and mythical legends.

Initially born in Akron, Ohio some 68 years ago... he heard many legends told around the campfire. Still, nothing like the tales the Aussies told, so he decided to gather the basics of the legends and develop them into stories that would prove the reputation Australia has - and that is that everything here wants to eat you. After reading his stories, you may believe that yourself.

Australian Elizabeth Waterhouse, assistant writer to R.E. Taylor in these Aussie Yarns, spends all her time trying to convince R.E. that her country welcomes all visitors to our shores with sunshine and Aussie hospitality, that Drop bears will not eat you alive. Yowies, Bunyips, and Marsupial Tigers are not an everyday occurrence!

Yet she also assures him that sharks, crocodiles, mosquitoes, and snakes are something to steer well clear of in her beautiful country - Australia. "Strewth, mate! Fair Dinkum, wait till you rub an Aussie Sheila the wrong way, or cop it from the bloody Tourist Industry!"

www.ingramcontent.com/pod-product-compliance
Lightning Source LLC
Chambersburg PA
CBHW061727070526
44583CB00024B/3030